My brethren, nothing teaches us so much the preciousness of the Creator as when we learn the emptiness of all besides. When you have been pierced through and through with the sentence, "Cursed is he that trusts in man, and makes flesh his arm," then will you suck unutterable sweetness from the divine assurance, "Blessed is he that trusts in the Lord, and whose hope the Lord is." Turning away with bitter scorn from earth's hives, where you found no honey, but many sharp stings, you will rejoice in Him whose faithful word is sweeter than honey or the honeycomb.[1] – Charles Spurgeon on Prayer

Confess your trespasses to one another, and pray for one another, that you may be healed. The effective, fervent prayer of a righteous man avails much (James 5:16, NKJV).

---

[1] Charles Spurgeon, Effective Prayer, Public Domain, spurgeongems.org.

TALKING

WITH

GOD

31 DAYS:
UNDERSTANDING PRAYER

DR. BRUCE HITCHCOCK

Printed in the United States of America

Published by Books for Ministry a 501(c)(3) tax-exempt nonprofit corporation. Providing spiritual growth materials to those who can least afford them.

For more information, see www.equippingchurches.net.

First Edition: 2023

ISBN-9798861150330

(Doctor of Commerce and Ministry, Honoris Causa, California Baptist University, 2017).

Table of Contents

Donor Information

The author's purpose is to produce books and other Christian tools that are biblically accurate, theologically sound, and useful for instruction in spiritual growth (2 Timothy 2:15, 2 Timothy 3:16-17). The salvation of unbelievers, the personal spiritual growth of believers, and the development of those who will disciple others in the future are paramount to the author (Psalms 71:18).

This book and the other books and materials published by this author are offered directly to consumers for a small donation to "Books for Ministry," a 501 (c)(3) LLC.

Free materials useful for those who are in recovery are available by emailing the author.

Books for Ministry" donates books to mentors who then use them to lead others to salvation and to disciple believers who cannot afford quality materials. We distribute our books in the United States and where possible, around the world.

For information on *BOOKS FOR MINISTRY*, to donate for this or other books by Dr. Hitchcock, or to make a direct donation, contact:

BOOKS FOR MINISTRY

Drbruceblog7@gmail.com

To purchase other books written by Dr. Hitchcock,

Google: Dr. Bruce Hitchcock Books

100% of all royalties are directly deposited into our non-prophet checking account.

1. QUESTION #1: WHAT IS PRAYER?

Matthew 7:7c

Opening Prayer:

Teach me your way, O Lord. Guide me as I walk in your truth. Allow my heart to be undivided, with You as its center. I will fear your name. I will praise you, O Lord my God. With all my heart, I will glorify your name forever. Great is your love toward me. You have delivered me from the fear of death. Thank You will not suffice. I must live a life reflecting Your grace. Let others see You in me O Lord. Let the testimony of my lips and the works of my hands honor only You my Savior. In Christ's perfect name, I pray. Amen! (Adapted from Psalms 86:11-13)!

Today's Bible Verse: Matthew 7:7c.

Knock, and it will be opened to you.

Associated Scriptures:

O Lord, open my lips, And my mouth shall show forth Your praise. For You do not desire sacrifice, or else I would give it; You do not delight in burnt offering. The sacrifices of God are a broken spirit, a broken and a contrite heart. These, O God, You will not despise (Psalms 51:15-17, NKJV).

Open to me the gates of righteousness; I will go through them, and I will praise the Lord. This is the gate of the Lord, through which the righteous shall enter. I will praise You, For You have answered me, And have become my salvation (Psalms 118:19-21).

Look upon me and be merciful to me, as Your custom is toward those who love Your name. Direct my steps by Your word, and let no iniquity have dominion over me. Redeem me from the oppression of man, that I may keep Your precepts (Psalms 119:132-134).

Correlative Quotes:

If you want to judge how well a person understands Christianity, find out how much he makes of the thought of being God's child, and having God as his father. If this is not the thought that prompts and controls his worship and prayers and his whole outlook on life, it means that he does not understand Christianity very well at all.[2] – J. I. Packer

Earlier in this sermon Jesus had given the disciples a model prayer. Now He assured them that God welcomes prayer and urged them to come to Him continuously and persistently. This is emphasized by the present tenses in the verbs: "keep on asking"; "keep on seeking"; "keep on knocking" (7:7). Why? Because your Father in heaven (v. 11) delights in giving good gifts (cf. James 1:17) to those who persist in prayer.[3] – Walvoord and Zuck

It used to be that only university professors believed in secularism, but with the advent of television and the rise of pop popular culture, The Enlightenment has made its way into the living room. It has captured the West, obscuring our view of what the world is really like Now, we see a flat, two-dimensional world that relegates God to the sidelines as a feel-good cheerleader. Prayer is private and personal, not public and real.[4] – Miller

---

[2] J. I. Packer, Knowing God, azguotes.com, Used by permission, Fair Use Authorization, Section 107, of the Copyright Law. P. 1.

[3] John Walvoord and Roy B. Zuck, The Bible Knowledge Commentary, N. T. Victor Books, Whitby, Ontario, Canada, Bucks, England, Used by permission, Fair Use Authorization, Section 107, of the Copyright Law.

[4] Paul E. Miller, A Praying Life, NavPress in alliance with Tyndale House publishers, Inc., Used by permission, Fair Use Authorization, Section 107, of the Copyright Law P. 105.

Author's Notes:

INTRODUCTION

As a young child, I remember my dad tucking my younger brother and me into bed each night. He would read us a story, and then we would say our prayers.

"Now I lay me down to sleep. I pray the Lord my soul to keep. If I should die before I wake, I pray the Lord my soul to take."

Prayer was a ritual.

We always prayed, thanking God before the evening meal. Whenever I visited any of my friends in the neighborhood for dinner, they also began the meal with a prayer of thanksgiving. Prayer was central and expected in all lives.

Historically, prayer has become a deeply ingrained and widespread practice across various religions and spiritual beliefs. The reasons why people pray are multifaceted. They can vary significantly depending on individual faiths and cultural contexts.

Fundamental Christianity believes a personal relationship with God is necessary to have prayers heard and answered. They understand and teach that non-believers do not have this relationship with God, and thus their prayers are never heard or answered as those of believers (John 9:31). Various interpretations of religious texts and teachings cannot change the truth of Scripture.

Using the word prayer with those outside the compass of fundamental Christianity can be confusing. A person who does not know Jesus as their personal Savior and Lord cannot contemplate the depth and closeness of our relationship with God. They, therefore, will not understand the comfort and joy we receive from answered prayer. Since they do not have the Spirit, they cannot receive answers from Him. Only through salvation do we have answered prayers. The God of Christianity does not understand the prayers of unbelievers. Isaiah 59:2 says: *But your iniquities have separated you from your God; your sins have hidden his face from you, so that he will not hear.*

Furthermore, John 9:31 explains: *We know that God does not listen to sinners. He listens to the godly person who does his will.*

THE CURRENT STATE OF PRAYER

Prayer has been an important of the fabric of American life since our inception. Since most early settlers came to our shores due to religious persecution, it only follows that they would be people of prayer.

Prayer remains the backbone of church services. Whether in traditional Christian churches or the newer Jesus movement congregations, prayers, either spoken or sung, remain a significant aspect of connecting with God.

We are still people who pray.

Additional findings from the survey include data measuring the share of Americans who connect with a higher power at 85%. The most frequently cited methods for connecting with a higher power include prayer (61%), meditation (39%), mindfulness (38%), the recitation of affirmation (30%) and spiritually based yoga (14%).

According to the survey, the average American prays twice a day and for 18 minutes every day. Eighty-four percent of those surveyed believe God hears their prayers regardless of how they believe.[5] - Foley

COMMUNICATING WITH GOD

Prayer is communicating with God. Verbal contact assumes interaction between two or more parties. When we pray, we commune with God, not talk to Him.

Communion with God implies a deeper and more intimate connection. It emphasizes the idea of spiritual union and communication with His divine presence. We talk to God through the divine presence of His Spirit, who lives in us.

ASPECTS OF THE COMMUNAL RELATIONSHIP

During prayer, believers open themselves up to the presence of God, seeking spiritual communion and a sense of unity with the Maker. We

---

[5] Ryan Foley, 87% of Americans Who Pray Say Prayers Were Answered in the Past Year., christianpost.com/news/87-percent-of-americans-who-pray-say-prayers-were-answered.html.,

achieve this connection to God through various forms of prayer, including petitionary prayers (asking for specific things), intercessory prayers (praying on behalf of others), prayers of thanksgiving, and contemplative prayers (meditative and reflective prayers).

The interpretation and practice of prayer can vary significantly across different religious traditions, denominations, and individual beliefs. Some believers may place a greater emphasis on the communal and meditative aspects of prayer, while others may focus more on specific requests and supplications. Ultimately, the nature and understanding of prayer are deeply influenced by an individual's faith, religious teachings, and personal experiences.

Prayer often becomes a last resort. When we have tried everything else, we finally seek God for help. Instead, talking to God should be our first reaction. If speaking to God were easy, or if we felt worthy, it would be as natural as communicating to our closest friend. He is!

It is time believers discover a deep and focused appreciation of our relationship with God. A study of prayer should include all factors regarding our communication with God. The first aspect of prayer discussed will focus on the question, What is prayer? God has established six types of prayer: petition, agreement, faith, dedication, intercession, and supplication. Each of these represents a singular way to communicate our desires to God.

The second concern will answer the query, Why do we pray? The general thought of prayer centers on our personal needs. However, these petitions for our affairs represent only a minor part of the need for prayer. We will go deeply into this question and explain not only our needs but also the needs of others. In addition, we will touch on our concern for worship through prayer, our praise of God, and the notion of thanksgiving to God.

Thirdly, we will ask, When should we pray? Timing is essential. The longer we wait to reach out to God, the less we show our faith in Him. Faith is a central issue in prayer. Appropriate initiation of our initial addresses and responses is of the essence. Our correspondence with God should be habitual.

Fourth, there will be an examination of the topic, How do we pray? In this part of our study, we will address the New Testament scripture found in Matthew 6:5-9. Here Jesus outlines five essentials for prayer. The best

11

teacher of prayer is God Himself. In this section of scripture, we see Christ's emphasis on the attitude of those who pray. We must approach God for the right reasons and in an appropriate manner.

Finally, we will discover, What do we pray for? In these chapters, we will complete the study of Christ's message on prayer in Matthew 6:10-18. We will see nine temporal and eternal concerns impacting all believers. These chief concerns influence us all. Prayer is not difficult. It is our goal to keep things simple. However, our communication with God requires a deeper understanding of Him and the restrictions and requirements placed on our relationship.

Spiritual Application:

Knock and it will be opened to you (Matthew 7:7c).

To *knock* means to reach out to God. This action is such a simple phrase but oh, how profound. To think we can open the door to a conversation with God only by reaching out to Him. Prayer is an entryway to a full and rewarding relationship with God. Through this door, we find salvation opening a new world of faith, hope, and love. We access all this through prayer.

Lessons within the Lesson:

List the thought-provoking verses or statements that spoke to you in this chapter.

Which statement may have the utmost impact on your prayer life?

How will your prayer life change because of this statement?

List the steps you will take to make the changes necessary to strengthen your prayer life.

2: PRAYER IN THE TRENCHES

Matthew 6:5-7 (NKJV)

<u>Opening Prayer</u>:

Great is Your Faithfulness

Great is Your faithfulness,
Kindness, and love,
Great are You Lord,
Your thrown sits above.

When we have faith,
You're always there.
And when we pray,
You always hear

You are the Sovereign,
Perfect and Right,
Yet you chose us to be,
Your love and delight

Nothing seems good enough,
For some of us,
We lack what we want,
We stew and we fuss.

Help us be patient,
To wait on Your grace.
Believing Your promises,
'til we meet face to face.

In the Son's name, we pray. Amen!

Today's Bible Verse: Matthew 6:5-7 (NKJV).

> *And when you pray, you shall not be like the hypocrites. For they love to pray standing in the synagogues and on the corners of the streets, that they may be seen by men. Assuredly, I say to you, they have their reward. But you, when you pray, go into your room, and when you have shut your door, pray to your Father who is in the secret place; and your Father who sees in secret will reward you openly. And when you pray, do not use vain repetitions as the heathens do. For they think that they will be heard for their many words.*

Associated Scriptures:

> *I do not sit with deceitful men, or do I consort with hypocrites; I abhor the assembly of evildoers and refuse to sit with the wicked* (Psalms 26:4-5).

> *You hypocrites! Isaiah was right when he prophesied about you: These people honor me with their lips, but their hearts are far from me.* (Matthew 15:7-9).

> *The secret things belong to the Lord our God, but the things revealed belong to us and to our children forever, that we may follow all the words of this law* (Deuteronomy 29:29).

Correlative Quotes:

Jesus then spoke about the practice of prayer, which the Pharisees loved to perform publicly. Rather than making prayer a matter between an individual and God, the Pharisees had turned it into an act to be seen by men - again, to demonstrate their supposed righteousness. Their prayers were directed not to God but to other men, and consisted of long, repetitive phrases (Matthew 6:7)[6] – Walvoord and Zuck.

Of course it is not the simple publicity of prayer which is here condemned. It may be offered in any circumstances, however open, if not prompted by the spirit of ostentation, but dictated

---

[6] John Walvoord and Roy B. Zuck, The Bible Knowledge Commentary, Ibid.

by the great ends of prayer itself. It is the retiring character of true prayer which is here taught.[7] – Jamieson, Fausset, Brown

The fact that a request is repeated does not make it a "vain repetition"; for both Jesus and Paul repeated their petitions (Matthew 26:36-46; 2 Corinthians 12:7-8). A request becomes a "vain repetition" if it is only a babbling of words without a sincere heart desire to seek and do God's will. The mere reciting of memorized prayers can be vain repetition. The Gentiles had such prayers in their pagan ceremonies (see 1 Kings 18:26).[8] – Wiersbe

Author's Notes:

INTRODUCTION: SALVATION IN JESUS:

The Gospel message is a clear and concise description of the relationship between humanity and its savior.

JESUS IS OUR RIGHTEOUSNESS

Romans 3:21-26 maintains:

> *But now a righteousness from God, apart from law, has been made known, to which the Law and the Prophets testify. This righteousness from God comes through faith in Jesus Christ to all who believe.*

JESUS JUSTIFIED HUMANITY THROUGH GOD'S GRACE

> *There is no difference, for all have sinned and fall short of the glory of God, and are justified freely by his grace through the redemption that came by Christ Jesus. God presented Him as a sacrifice of atonement, through faith in His blood. He did this to demonstrate His justice, because in His forbearance (Mercy) He had left the sins committed beforehand unpunished. He did it to demonstrate His justice at the present time, so as to be*

---

[7] Robert Jamieson, A.R. Fausset, David Brown, Commentary Critical and Explanatory on the Whole Bible, Public Domain 1871, Public Domain, Copy Freely, P. 25.

[8] Warren Wiersbe, The Wiersbe Bible Commentary: New Testament,bethelchurchmuncie.files. wordpress.com/2020/07/wiersbe-commentary-new-testament.pdf, Used by permission, Fair Use Authorization, Section 107, of the Copyright Law, P. 22.

just and the One who justifies those who have faith in Jesus (Romans 3:25-26).

JESUS GIVES THE ABUNDANT LIFE TO THOSE WHO BELIEVE

In John 10:7-10, Jesus testifies to the life His chosen have in Christ when He explains:

> *I tell you the truth, I am the gate for the sheep. All who ever came before Me were thieves and robbers, but the sheep did not listen to them. I am the gate; whoever enters through Me will be saved. He will come in and go out, and find pasture. The thief comes only to steal and kill and destroy; I have come that they may have life and have it more abundantly.*

HE GUARANTEES ETERNAL LIFE

All believers have eternal life in Jesus. The adage *Once saved, always saved* is as accurate today as it was when originally coined. God's grace is complete.

In Acts 2:38:

> *Peter replied, 'Repent and be baptized, every one of you, in the name of Jesus Christ for the forgiveness of your sins. And you will receive the gift of the Holy Spirit.*

Salvation through Christ is also unconditional. Ephesians 4:32 teaches:

> *Be kind and compassionate to one another, forgiving each other, just as in Christ God forgave you.*

Salvation is a gift from God, not something we can earn or lose by human efforts. The Father's forgiveness is complete. Christ's sacrifice on the cross covers all past, present, and future sins committed by the believer (Romans 8:38-39).

WE ARE SEALED UNTIL THE DAY OF REDEMPTION

The Spirit has sealed us for eternity. In Ephesians 1:13, Paul teaches:

> *And you also were included in Christ when you heard the message of truth, the gospel of your salvation. When*

you believed, you were marked in him with a seal, the
promised Holy Spirit.

JESUS HELPS OVERCOME UNHEALTHY LIFE DECISIONS

We must note that *Life in Christ* does not guarantee perfection or immunity from making mistakes, as all humans are fallible. However, faith in Christ will provide strength and resources to overcome unhealthy patterns and pursue a more purposeful and fulfilling life.

Life in Christ refers to the transformative relationship believers experience with Jesus Christ after accepting Him as their Lord and Savior. This relationship is central to the Christian since it ignites spiritual growth, moral development, and positive changes in a believer's life.

JESUS HELPS US OVERCOME TEMPTATION.

Resistance to temptation refers to deliberately and steadfastly avoiding or overcoming the allure of engaging in actions bearing on moral or ethical principles. Our continued righteousness involves the ability to make conscious choices and exercise self-control. When faced with situations that may entice individuals to act in immoral ways, failure seems imminent. The regenerate and unregenerate recognize these actions as wrong, harmful, and contrary to their values.

The ability to overcome the allurements of this world receives its power from the Holy Spirit. Resistance is futile without His power.

Unbelievers cannot overcome the enticements and societal pressures associated with them. Proverbs 26:11 states: As a dog returns to its vomit, fools repeat their folly.

Through prayer, study of the Bible, and seeking the guidance of the Holy Spirit, believers will receive wisdom and discernment to make better life choices. Knowledge, understanding, wisdom, application, and repetition are the keys to spiritual growth. These essentials allow His children to seek alignment in their decisions using God's will and biblical principles.

Prayer provides the foundation for the action of spiritual growth. Growth in our Savior is generated through the conversations we have with God and provide the conduit through which we receive our instruction.

Communication with the Trinity establishes and encourages our resistance to temptation. Our age as a believer is not determined by how long ago we believed in Jesus. It is instead, a measure of the extent of your spiritual growth.

JESUS ENCOURAGES PRAYER

Our new relationship with Jesus encourages us to be people of prayer. Prayer is an essential part of our spiritual growth and relationship with God. Through our communication with Him we begin to understand the reality and depth of His love for us. As we experience the intimacy of our relationship, we begin to understand His caring nature. He will always hear us and answer our petitions according to His will for us.

Spiritual Application:

God not only desires our prayers, he demands them. Philippians 4:6 states: *Be anxious for nothing, but in everything by prayer and supplication with thanksgiving let your requests be made known to God.*

Prayer in the Trenches recognizes the importance and unconditional nature of our appeals. We accept God's willingness to answer prayer and encourage his faithfulness by continuing to ask. The action of salvation paves the way for God to show His power in all things. We praise His goodness and grace.

Lessons within the Lesson:

List the thought-provoking verses or statements that spoke to you in this chapter.

Which statement may have the utmost impact on your prayer life?

How will your prayer life change because of this statement?

List the steps you will take to make the changes necessary to strengthen your prayer life.

3: FORMAL PRAYER

1 Samuel 2:1

Opening Prayer: (Today's prayer is adapted from Psalms 54:1-6)

Save me, O God, by Your name. Vindicate me by Your might. Hear my prayer, O God. Listen to the words of my mouth. An unbelieving world attacks me relentlessly. Ruthless people seek my testimony. Those without regard for God sear my flesh. Selah. You are my help and stay, O Lord. You are the one who sustains me. Let evil recoil on those who slander me. In Your faithfulness to me, turn them aside. Give my victory over the enemies of righteousness, O Lord. Hear my prayer O God. It is in the Lamb's sacrificial and holy name we pray. Amen!

Today's Bible Verse: **1 Samuel 2:1.**

My heart rejoices in the LORD; in the LORD my horn is lifted high. My mouth boasts over my enemies, for I delight in your deliverance.

Associated Scriptures:

Serve the Lord with fear and rejoice with trembling. Kiss the Son, lest he be angry and you be destroyed in your way, for his wrath can flare up in a moment. Blessed are all who take refuge in him (Psalms 2:11-12).

I will be glad and rejoice in your love, for you saw my affliction and knew the anguish of my soul. You have not handed me over to the enemy but have set my feet in a spacious place (Psalms 31:7-8).

Let the righteous rejoice in the Lord and take refuge in him; let all the upright in heart praise him (Psalms 64:10).

Correlative Quotes:

Hannah, with clear reference to her rival Peninnah, spoke of her joy in the LORD who had helped her achieve satisfaction at last. Horns, used by animals for defense and attack, symbolized strength. Thus, Hannah spoke of her horn in describing the strength that had come to her because God had answered her prayer.[9] – Walvoord and Zuck

It's good for us to begin our praying with praising, because praise helps us focus on the glory of the Lord and not on the greatness of our needs. When we see the greatness of God, we start to see life in perspective. Hannah knew the character of God and exalted His glorious attributes. She began by affirming His holiness and uniqueness.[10] – Wiersbe

Praise and prayer are inseparably conjoined in Scripture. (Colossians 4.2; I Timothy 2. 1.) This beautiful song was her tribute of thanks for the divine goodness in answering her petition, .[11] – Jamison, Fawcett, and Brown

Author's Notes:

INTRODUCTION

Formal prayer refers to structured and prescribed prayers that are part of established religious traditions and practices. Many of these prayers come from the Bible and magnify and glorify God. They often have specific wording and may be recited in a set manner, either individually or collectively during worship. Formal prayers are an essential part of the worship experience for believers.

---

[9] John Walvoord and Roy B. Zuck, The Bible Knowledge Commentary, O. T., Victor Books, Whitby, Ontario, Canada, Bucks, England, Used by permission, Fair Use Authorization, Section 107, of the Copyright Law., P. 334.

[10] Warren Wiersbe, The Wiersbe Bible Commentary: O.T.,bethelchurchmuncie.files. wordpress.com/2020/07/wiersbe-commentary-new-testament.pdf, Used by permission, Fair Use Authorization, Section 107, of the Copyright Law., P. 497.

[11] Robert Jamieson, A.R. Fausset, David Brown, Commentary Critical and Explanatory on the Whole Bible O. T. Vol II, Public Domain 1871, P. 176.

Informal prayer, also known as spontaneous or personal prayer, refers to a type of prayer that is not structured or prescribed by any specific religious tradition. Unlike formal prayers, which often have set wording and follow a particular format, informal prayer is more spontaneous and individualized. It involves speaking directly to God or expressing thoughts, feelings and needs equally personal and unrehearsed. Informal pray is talking with God.

FORMAL PRAYER:

Formal prayer is a composite of one or more of the following elements. These characteristics of reserved appeal suggest position, praise, promise, possession, petition, and proclamation.

Hanna's tribute to God at the birth of her son Samuel (1 Samuel 2:1-10) represents an example of formal prayer. She incorporates all the elements constituting worship and thankfulness. They represent the essence of formally reaching out to the Creator.

POSITION: GOD IS HOLY

1 Samuel 2:2 states:

> *There is no one holy like the Lord; there is no one besides you; there is no Rock like our God.*

Hanah identifies God's position in three words. He is Holy. Holiness means completeness in righteousness and justice. God defines completeness. He does not evolve. Secondly, the Divine is unique. No one can compare to God. Finally, He is the Rock. The Creator of all things does not change. His nature is permanently the same.

PRAISE: GOD IS WORTHY OF OUR ADORATION

1 Samuel 2:1 Demonstrates God's praiseworthiness:

> *My heart rejoices in the Lord; in the Lord, my horn is lifted high. My mouth boasts over my enemies, for I delight in your deliverance.*

The word horn refers to the strength of the oxen's horn, their weapon of choice. This portion of the comprehensive prayer pictures her gratitude as she gives God credit for the pregnancy and delivery.

PROMISE

In the account of 1 Samuel 1:12-17, we see the interaction between Eli, the prophet, and Hannah:

As she kept on praying to the Lord, Eli observed her mouth. Hannah was praying in her heart, and her lips were moving but her voice was not heard. Eli thought she was drunk and said to her, How long will you keep on getting drunk? Get rid of your wine.

Hannah defends herself by explaining to Eli her commitment to God:

Not so, my lord, Hannah replied, I am a woman who is deeply troubled. I have not been drinking wine or beer; I was pouring out my soul to the Lord. Do not take your servant for a wicked woman; I have been praying here out of my great anguish and grief.

Eli, the prophet of God, with great authority makes this interesting statement: *Eli answered, Go in peace, and may the God of Israel grant you what you have asked of him.*

Eli's response, *may the God of Israel grant you what you have asked of him*, indicates the prophet's knowledge that God heard Hannah's prayer and her request would be granted.[12]

POSSESSION

1 Samuel 1:19-20 defines the element of possession in prayer.

Early the next morning they arose and worshipped before the Lord and then went back to their home at Ramah. Elkanah lay with Hannah his wife, and the Lord remembered her. So in the course of time Hannah conceived and gave birth to a son. She named him Samuel, saying, "Because I asked the Lord for him.

---

[12] Matthew Henry, Vol. II, Matthew Henry, An Exposition of the Old and New Testament (Unabridged), Volume II (Joshua-Esther), Public Domain, Philadelphia : Ed. Harrington & Geo. D. Haswell, Market Street,1706, bitimage.dyndns. org/., P. 229.

To believe God will answer means living as if the request was fulfilled. To possess something means it already belongs to you. Anticipation in the form of handwringing should not exist in prayer. To ask in God's will means to expect we will receive our request. Jesus says in Mark 11:24:

> Therefore I tell you, whatever you ask for in prayer, believe that you have received it, and it will be yours.

The mature Christian petitions God and then believes He will answer the prayer in the proper way with exact timing. He knows the desires of our hearts (Psalm 37:4). Philippians 4:19 states unequivocally:

> And my God will meet all your needs according to the riches of his glory in Christ Jesus.

PETITION

Petitioning God, also known as prayer of petition or supplication, is a type of prayer where individuals or communities make specific requests or pleas to the Father.

They ask for help, guidance, or intervention. In this appeal, people bring their needs, desires, and concerns before the Godhead and ask for assistance or blessings in various aspects of life.

Hanna's petition in 1 Samuel 1:11a was simple: *O Lord Almighty, if you will only look upon your servant's misery.*

In her prayer, Hannah recognizes God as Lord. She addresses Him as being almighty, the only God above all. Hannah introduces herself as being sad and experiencing distress. She cries out to her Maker for recognition and sympathy, giving her a request for a son.

Hannah promises to dedicate the boy to God for His service. She has included the elements of formal prayer in one brief statement. We do not have to be eloquent in our language when we petition God.

He knows our hearts. He hears our words. He knows our motives.

PROCLAMATION

Hannah concludes Her prayer with this statement in 1 Samuel 2:11b: *Remember me, and do not forget your servant but give her a son,*

23

then I will give him to the Lord for all the days of his life, and no razor will ever be used on his head.

In the correct order, this proclamation of her barren position precedes the promise of dedicating the boy to God for His purposes.

> Let it be definitely accepted among us Christian people that, whatever the difficulty is, whatever shape it takes, secular or sacred, Men ought always to pray, that is, they ought to pray about everything.

> This is the remedy that will cure all diseases; this is the sword that shall cut the Gordian knot if it cannot be untied; this is the key that fits the wards of every lock in the prison-house of our sorrow. We shall get clean out if we do but know how to use the key to prayer. Men ought always to pray.[13] – Spurgeon

Spiritual Application:

Hannah's petition to her Maker typifies the formal prayer. These formal prayers serve as a means of expressing devotion, seeking guidance, offering gratitude, and fostering a deeper connection with the Creator in various religious traditions. Formal prayer recognizes God as being the Maker of everything, the Master of all things, the Manager of everything in existence, and the Maintainer. He expects to be recognized for His Greatness (1 Chronicles 29:11). Formal prayer accomplishes our desire to give Him the recognition the Godhead deserves.

Lessons within the Lesson:

List the thought-provoking verses or statements that spoke to you in this chapter.

Which statement may have the utmost impact on your prayer life?

How will your prayer life change because of this statement?

List the steps you will take to make the changes necessary to strengthen your prayer life.

---

[13] Charles Spurgeon, When Should We Pray, Public Domain, spurgeon.org/resource-library/sermons/when-should-we-pray/#flipbook/. P. 1.

24

4: THE LORD'S PRAYER

Matthew 6:9-13

Opening Prayer:

Help us, O Lord, to love You more each day. Convict us to pray without ceasing as You have commanded in Your Word. Keep us mindful to follow the designs of Your Word when we open our hearts. Do not allow the temptations of this world to interfere with our close contact with You at all times. In Jesus' name, we pray. Amen!

Today's Bible Verse: Matthew 6:9-13 (NKJV).

In this manner, therefore, pray: Our Father in heaven, Hallowed be Your name. Your kingdom come. Your will be done on earth as it is in heaven. Give us this day our daily bread. And forgive us our debts, as we forgive our debtors. And do not lead us into temptation, but deliver us from the evil one. For Yours is the kingdom and the power and the glory forever. Amen.

Associated Scriptures:

Be clear minded and self-controlled so that you can pray (1 Peter 4:7).

Is any one of you in trouble? He should pray. Is anyone happy? Let him sing songs of praise (James 5:13).

The prayer of a righteous man is powerful and effective

(James 5:16).

<u>**Correlative Quotes**</u>:

> She had by prayer committed her case to God, and left it with him, and now she was no more perplexed about it.[14] – Henry

> Prayer should be addressed to your Father, who is unseen (John 1:18; 1 Timothy 1:17) and who knows what you need; it is not to be seen by men.[15] – Walvoord and Zuck

> But it is wrong to pray in public if we are not in the habit of praying in private. Observers may think that we are practicing prayer when we are not, and this is hypocrisy.[16] – Wiersbe

<u>**Author's Notes**</u>:

INTRODUCTION

We can pray as Hannah prayed. There are many examples in the Bible. The Lord's Prayer is the most common. It is found in Matthew 6:9-13 (NKJV):

> *Jesus commanded: In this manner, therefore, pray.*

Jesus uses The Lord's Prayer as a spiritual template or formula for formal prayer. In the NKJV, CSB, we read: In this manner therefore pray. He is saying pray like this. The NIV version begins: This then is HOW you should pray. This statement becomes an example of prayer. Jesus doesn't say, this is what you should pray. In the NASB version of the text, it reads: Pray then in this way. Finally, in the Loving Bible, the phrase says: Pray along these lines.

PRAY RECOGNIZING GOD'S HOLINESS: MATTHEW 6:9

> *Our Father in heaven, Hallowed be Your name.*

God is not like humanity. He is perfect in all ways. The Creator's nature makes Him the author and protector of righteousness. Numbers 23:19 states: *God is not human, that he should lie, not a human being, that he should change his mind.*

We can trust God completely because He is absolute holiness.

---

[14] Matthew Henry, Vol. II, Matthew Henry, An Exposition of the Old and New Testament (Unabridged), Volume II (Joshua-Esther), Public Domain, Ibid. P. 229.

[15] John Walvoord and Roy B. Zuck, The Bible Knowledge Commentary, N. T., Ibid.

[16] Warren Wiersbe, The Wiersbe Bible Commentary: New Testament, Ibid., P. 22.

Isaiah 6:1-3 allows us an inside look at the one who controls everything. It reads in part: *I saw the Lord sitting on a throne, high and lifted, and the train of His robe filled the temple. Above it stood seraphim. And one cried to another and said: Holy, holy, holy is the Lord of hosts; The whole earth is full of His glory!*

We see God as Holy. We fall short of His holiness (Romans 5:8). We also see the New Testament teaching us in Titus 1:1-2: *Paul, a servant of God and an apostle of Jesus Christ, to further the faith of God's elect and their knowledge of the truth that leads to godliness, in the hope of eternal life, which God, WHO DOES NOT LIE, promised before the beginning of time.*

PRAY FOR CHRIST'S RETURN

Your kingdom come. Your will be done on earth as it is in heaven (Matthew 6:10*).*

Jesus promised He would return. In Matthew 24:37, Jesus said: *As it was in the days of Noah, so it will be at the coming of the Son of Man.* I saw a bumper sticker that said: Jesus is coming again — This time, He's mad.

PRAY FOR YOUR NEEDS: Matthew 6:11:

Give us this day our daily bread,

God's word contains a trifecta of verses concerning believers' needs. Everything we must know about His ability to care for us we find in these verses.

Jesus will provide for our basic needs. 2 Corinthians 9:8 (ESV) teaches us: *And God is able to make all grace abound to you, so that having all sufficiency in all things at all times, you may abound in every good work.*

The promises continue in 1 Petr 5:7 (ESV), where the apostle writes: *Casting all your anxieties on him because he cares for you. All means all.* Nothing can extricate or separate us from our life in Christ Jesus. Matthew 6:31 (ESV) explains: *Therefore, do not be anxious, saying, What shall we eat? or What shall we drink? or What shall we wear? Christians, too often, allow the distractions of this world to inhibit our walk with God. Fear seems to be the greatest of these hindrances. Don't let fear weaken you.*

PRAY FOR THE FORGIVENESS OF SIN: Matthew 6:12:

> *And forgive us our debts* (Trespasses), *As we forgive our debtors* (those who trespass against us).

To maintain our spiritual growth, we must live in the light (1 John 1:7). Living in the light includes repenting when we sin (1 John 1:9).

PRAY FOR PROTECTION AGAINST TEMPTATION: Matthew 6:13a.

> *And do not lead us into temptation,*

The world system will try drawing us in to be like them; destitute. We must resist using the power found in prayer. Jesus, being tempted in the wilderness by Satan, used scripture and prayer to win the victory. We will live a spiritually victorious life when following His example (Matthew 4:1-11)

PRAY FOR PROTECTION AGAINST ALL EVIL: Matthew 6:13b.

But deliver us from the evil one. This statement by Jesus gives us a carte blanche against evil. Our Lord is inviting us to use His name to ward off all evil.

Spiritual Application:

> *For if you forgive men their trespasses, your heavenly Father will also forgive you. But if you do not forgive men their trespasses, neither will your Father forgive your trespasses* (Matthew 6:14-15).

Jesus suggests, as He completes The Lord's Prayer, we consider forgiving the sins of others. The little word *if* gives us a choice. However, our selection carries a warning. His promise has eternal significance.

Lessons within the Lesson:

List the thought-provoking verses or statements that spoke to you in this chapter.

Which statement may have the utmost impact on your prayer life?

How will your prayer life change because of this statement?

List the steps you will take to make the changes necessary to strengthen your prayer life.

5: INFORMAL PRAYER

John 15:7

Opening Prayer: (The opening prayer is adapted from Psalms 51:15-19).

O Lord, open my lips, and my mouth will declare your praise. You no longer require blood sacrifices, or I would bring an offering to You. Offerings to You, O God, include a broken spirit, a remorseful attitude, and a repentant heart. You will not despise these tributes. In Your time and by Your resolve, make us prosper; build up the walls of our resistance to temptation. Then there will be righteous sacrifices to delight you. Then our lives will embrace Your grace. We will offer ourselves a personal offering. We will become wholly acceptable in Your sight. O Lord, You are our strength and redeemer. In the Lord's name, we pray. Amen!

Today's Bible Verse: John 15:7.

If you remain in me and my words remain in you, ask whatever you wish, and it will be done for you.

Associated Scriptures:

The elder, To my dear friend Gaius, whom I love in the truth. Dear friend, I pray that you may enjoy good health and that all may go well with you, even as your soul is getting along well (3 John 1-2).

The end of all things is near. Therefore, be clear minded and self-controlled so that you can pray (Peter 4:7).

Therefore, confess your sins to each other and pray for

each other so that you may be healed. The prayer of a righteous man is powerful and effective (James 5:16).

Correlative Quotes:

Always pray and not give up (Luke 18:1). If men ought to pray, they may pray. Whatever a man ought to do, it is clear that he has the right and the privilege to do; and though this may seem a very common-place truth to those of us whose hearts are at ease through faith in Jesus, and who enjoy daily communion with God in prayer, yet there is an exquisite sweetness about this fact to a man who fears that he may not pray. But our text says, *Men ought always to pray.* Then, men may always pray.[17] – Spurgeon

How can we Christians ever be discouraged and frustrated when we already share the glory of God? Our suffering today only guarantees that much more glory when Jesus Christ returns![18] – Wiersbe

Once again, ask for what you want, seek for what you have lost, knock for that from which you are excluded. Perhaps this last arrangement best indicates the shades of meaning and brings out the distinctions. Ask for everything you need, whatever it may be, if it is a right and good thing, it is promised to the sincere asker.[19] – Spurgeon

Author's Notes:

INTRODUCTION

The word translated as ask in John 15:7 accentuates our ability to come before our Creator with any requests. God answers every prayer. However, our Lord does not always give us what we want. The open door to the Father grants us the right to come into the Presence of God.

The crucifixion of Christ opened the curtain guarding the Holy of Holies. His payment ripped the temple drape in two. The place only

---

[17] Charles Spurgeon, Why Then Should We Pray?, spurgeon.org/resource-library/sermons/when-should-we-pray/#flipbook/, Public Domain, P. 1.

[18] Warren Wiersbe, The Wiersbe Bible Commentary: New Testament, Ibid, P. 431.

[19] Charles Spurgeon, Knock, sermon #1723, spurgeongems.org Public Domain, P. 2.

available to the High Priest of Israel is now open to every believer. Just as the High Priest did not receive all he desired, neither will we.

CHARACTERISTICS OF INFORMAL PRAYER

FERVENT PRAYER:

> *Be kindly affectionate to one another with brotherly love, in honor giving preference to one another; not lagging in diligence, fervent in spirit, serving the Lord; rejoicing in hope, patient in tribulation, continuing steadfastly in prayer; distributing to the needs of the saints, given to hospitality* (Romans 12:10-13).

Informal prayer must still be considered fervent prayer. No prayer should be flippant. Fervent prayer means intense and passionate prayer characterized by deep sincerity, earnestness, and robust emotions. It is a form of prayer where individuals express their deepest desires, feelings, and needs with great passion and dedication.

Fervent prayers often mark an overwhelming sense of urgency and a wholehearted desire to connect with our Father profoundly and intimately.

All prayer should be fervent and reverent. We owe it to God and to ourselves to show emotion and humility to our Father.

PERSONAL AND UNSCRIPTED:

> *May these words of my mouth and this meditation of my heart be pleasing in your sight, LORD, my Rock and my Redeemer* (Psalm 19:14).

Although many prayers have been written to be repeated by Christians to fulfill the obligation to pray, informal prayers emanate from the speaker's personal words. They reflect unique thoughts, emotions, and experiences. There are no fixed phrases or prescribed language. These informal utterances come directly from the heart to God through His Spirit.

> *Then I prayed to the God of heaven, and I answered the king, If it pleases the king and if your servant has found favor in his sight, let him send me to the city in Judah where my fathers are buried so that I can rebuild it* (Nehemiah 2:4-5)

Unlike formal prayers with set formats, informal prayers can take any form and vary in length and content.

A Canaanite woman came to Jesus and cried: *Lord, Son of David, have mercy on me! My daughter is demon-possessed and suffering terribly.* The disciples tried to dissuade her. She was undaunted. The woman came and knelt before Him. "*Lord, help me!*" she said. Jesus answered her prayer.

These two prayers to Jesus were different in length and structure. Both expressed faith. Faith healed the daughter. Jesus became the conduit through her belief. Size and profoundness of expression did not matter.

EMOTIONAL:

Evening, morning and noon I cry out in distress, and he hears my voice (Psalms 55:17).

Informal prayers often involve expressing a wide range of emotions. Joy, gratitude, sorrow, confusion, and many others may dominate the subjects of our petitions to our Lord. As individuals share their innermost feelings with Jesus, tears often wet the face of those in need. Tears can express joy and sorrow. Whether we pray from a needful or thankful heart, God accepts our innermost feeling.

SPONTANEOUS:

O LORD, our Lord, how majestic is your name in all the earth! You have set your glory in the heavens (Psalm 8:1).

King David's outburst in Psalm 8:1 was a spontaneous cry to the God he loved. Spontaneous prayers, sometimes known as extemporaneous or improvised prayers, are offered in the moment without premeditated or rehearsed words.

They are heartfelt expressions of communication with the divine, spoken directly from believers' thoughts and emotions at that particular time. Unlike formal prayers, which may have set wording and follow a structured format, spontaneous prayers are unscripted and flow naturally from the person praying.

FLEXIBLE:

I hold fast to your statutes, Lord; do not let me be put to shame. I run in the path of your commands, for you have broadened my understanding (Psalm 119.31-32, NIV).

Since informal prayers are not bound by rigid rules, individuals can pray anywhere and anytime, whether alone or in the presence of others. Time sometimes allows us to pray in seclusion in our hidden place. However, there are occasions when we must pray on the run. We then may use a flexible prayer style. Lord, I need your help now! Since God already knows your need, you may not have time to spell it out. Be flexible.

CONVERSATIONS WITH GOD:

The Lord is near to all who call on Him, to all who call on Him in truth. He fulfills the desires of those who fear Him; He hears their cry and saves them. The Lord watches over all who love Him, but all the wicked He will destroy. My mouth will speak in praise of the Lord. Let every creature praise his holy name for ever and ever (Psalms 145:18-2).

Informal prayer is akin to a one-on-one conversation with our Lord and Savior, expressing our thoughts and seeking comfort, guidance, or understanding. Every informal pray should involve a conversation with God. Formal prayers generally follow a set pattern, but informal prayer should be just that, informal.

AUTHENTIC:

In everything give thanks (1 Thessalonians 5:18, NKJV).

Informal prayers are often seen as more authentic and heartfelt, as they stem from a genuine and sincere connection between the individual and the Divine.

Authentic prayers refer to prayers that come from a place of genuineness, sincerity, and honesty. These prayers are heartfelt and express the true thoughts, emotions, and desires of the person praying. In authentic prayers, individuals are open and transparent with themselves and the Divine, sharing their innermost feelings, joys, struggles, and hopes without pretense or artifice.

I was playing golf on a hot and muggy day. The perspiration was running down my back. I said, Lord we could use a little breeze. Suddenly, there was a cool breeze on a summer day. Immediately I responded, Thank you Lord for the cool breeze. I could have thanked the ocean. I could have shown gratitude to mother nature. I could have thought it was a coincidence. I have learned, as I grow spiritually, there are no coincidences with God. He hears and He answers.

Spiritual Application:

Informal prayer means speaking with God person to person. The word *with* is critical to the understanding of these prayers. Believers do not talk at or to God. We talk with Him through the Holy Spirit. It is wrong to demand answers to prayers. Since He expects the believer to be humble in their demeanor, the Creator will not answer their demands. The emphasis of informal prayer is on the grace of God for keeping His promises. We must always approach God with the honor He deserves.

Informal prayers are common in Christian traditions. We offered them in private and public settings. They may be said silently in our minds or spoken out loud. Many people find comfort and solace in this form of prayer, as they provide an immediate and unfiltered means of communicating with our Lord and expressing their innermost thoughts and emotions.

Lessons within the Lesson:

List the thought-provoking verses or statements that spoke to you in this chapter.

Which statement may have the utmost impact on your prayer life?

How will your prayer life change because of this statement?

List the steps you will take to make the changes necessary to strengthen your prayer life.

6: PRAYERS OF PETITION

Matthew 26.39

Opening Prayer:

May you be blessed by the Lord, the Maker of heaven and earth. The highest heavens belong to the Lord, but the earth he has given to man. It is not the dead who praise the Lord, those who go down to silence; it is we who extol the Lord, both now and forevermore. Praise be Your name forever and ever (adapted from Psalms 115:15-18). In the Savior's name, we pray. Amen!

Today's Bible Verse: Matthew 26.39.

My Father, if it is possible, may this cup be taken from me. Yet not as I will, but as you will.

Associated Scriptures:

"Take this cup of the wine of wrath from My hand and cause all the nations to whom I send you to drink it. They will drink and stagger and go mad because of the sword that I will send among them." Then I took the cup from the Lord's hand and made all the nations to whom the Lord sent me drink it (Jeremiah 25:15-17, NASB).

Babylon has been a golden cup in the hand of the Lord, Intoxicating all the earth. The nations have drunk of her wine; therefore, the nations are going mad (Jeremiah 51:7, NASB).

He also will drink of the wine of the wrath of God, which is mixed in full strength in the cup of His anger; and he will be tormented with fire and brimstone in the presence of the holy angels and in the presence of the Lamb (Revelation 14:10, NASB).

Correlative Quotes:

Separating Himself then from the three, He prayed to His Father, asking that if... possible... this cup be taken away from Him. The "cup" probably referred to His imminent death. He also may have had in mind His coming separation from the Father (27:46)[20]– Walvoord and Zuck

Jesus was not wrestling with God's will or resisting God's will. He was yielding Himself to God's will. As perfect Man, He felt the awful burden of sin, and His holy soul was repelled by it. Yet as the Son of God, He knew that this was His mission in the world. The mystery of His humanity and deity is seen vividly in this scene.[21] – Wiersbe

We cannot even imagine the horror he felt when that sin was placed upon him. It was a horrendous experience for this one who was holy. Notice that he was not asking to escape the cross, but he was praying that God's will be done.[22] – McGee

Author's Notes:

INTRODUCTION

Prayers of petition, also known as supplication or intercessory prayers, describe the requests by individuals or people groups making specific submissions or pleas to a Higher Power.

In Christianity, God represents power. Our requests come to our Father through the Son. They are channeled to the Son by the Holy Spirit. He knows the thoughts of God's children and interprets them into heavenly language.

Romans 8:26 explains: *The Spirit helps us in our weakness. We do not know what we ought to pray for, but the Spirit himself intercedes for us*

---

[20] John Walvoord and Roy B. Zuck, The Bible Knowledge Commentary, N. T., Ibid.

[21] Warren Wiersbe, The Wiersbe Bible Commentary: N. T., Ibid., P. 79.

[22] J. Vernon McGee, Through the Bible with J. Vernon McGee, Vol. III, Proverbs-Malachi, Used by permission, Fair Use Authorization, Section 107, of the Copyright Law, P. 141.

through wordless groans. Through the power and language of the Spirit and these prayers, people seek assistance, guidance, or intervention for themselves or others in various aspects of life.

Petitionary prayers have become the most common form to petition the creator across different religions and spiritual traditions. Christianity offers no exception.

To petition means to ask God for something. The most famous ask in scripture is when Jesus said in Matthew 26.39: *My Father if it is possible, may this cup be taken from me. Yet not as I will, but as you will.*

KEY ELEMENTS OF PRAYERS OF PETITION:

SPECIFIC REQUESTS:

Petitionary prayers involve making specific requests to our Lord. These requests can be for personal needs, such as health, protection, or success, or they can be on behalf of others, seeking blessings, healing, or support for someone else.

> *But the Lord is faithful. He will establish you and guard you against the evil one. But the Lord is faithful. He will establish you and guard you against the evil one* (2 Thessalonians 3:3, ESV).

EXPRESSION OF NEEDS AND DESIRES:

In this type of prayer, individuals openly share their desires, concerns, and challenges with the higher power. They communicate their hopes and wishes, laying them before the Divine.

> *Peace I leave with you; my peace I give you. I do not give to you as the world gives. Do not let your hearts be troubled and do not be afraid* (John 14:27).

TRUST AND FAITH:

Petitioners approach the Higher Power with an understanding of trust and faith that their prayers will be heard and answered. They believe in the benevolence and responsiveness of the Divine One.

> *Every good and perfect gift is from above, coming down from the Father of the heavenly lights, who does not change like shifting shadows.* (James 1:17).

HUMILITY AND REVERENCE:

While expressing their desires, those offering prayers of petition should demonstrate humility and reverence before the Creator of all things, including humanity. They acknowledge the greatness and authority of the Divine Creator, Jesus.

> *Praise the LORD, my soul. LORD my God, you are very great; you are clothed with splendor and majesty.* (Psalm 104:1).

UNDERSTANDING THE DIVINE WILL:

While presenting their requests, individuals may also acknowledge that Our Heavenly Father's responses to our prayers may not always align with personal wishes. He gives believers what they need, not necessarily what they want. His gifts and promises to demonstrate His great love for us. We must demonstrate a willingness to accept whatever outcome the Trinity deems best.

> *If you then, who are evil, know how to give good gifts to your children, how much more will your Father who is in heaven give good things to those who ask him!* (Matthew 7:11).

GRATITUDE AND PRAISE:

Sometimes, prayers of petition include expressions of gratitude and praise to the Higher Power for past blessings and favors received.

> *May the God of peace, who through the blood of the eternal covenant brought back from the dead our Lord Jesus, that great Shepherd of the sheep, equip you with everything good for doing his will, and may he work in us what is pleasing to him, through Jesus Christ, to whom be glory for ever and ever. Amen* (Hebrews 13:20-21).

Petitionary prayers can be private and individual or shared collectively within a community during religious gatherings or events. They provide a means for people to seek comfort, support, and hope in times of difficulty and to feel connected to something larger than themselves.

A prayer of petition characterizes a specific type of prayer. An individual believer or group of Christians makes a formal request to God. Petitioners seek assistance, guidance, or intervention regarding shared needs or desires. The focus is on asking for something, be it for oneself or on behalf of others.

The structure and content of a prayer or petition may vary based on religious or spiritual traditions, but they typically include the following elements. Differing cultures of believers may use contrasting, distinct methods of reaching out to God.

ADDRESSING A DIVINE MAKER

A prayer usually begins by addressing God verbally. This form of praying can be done through various titles or names associated with the Divine being, expressing reverence and acknowledgment of His authority. We should address God like Thomas did when He saw Jesus and exclaimed:

Thomas said to him, My Lord and my God! (John 20:28).

EXPRESSION OF NEEDS

Petitioners clearly state the specific needs or desires for the help or intervention they seek. These needs range from personal concerns like health, safety, or success. They may also focus on broader issues such as peace, justice, or healing for others.

Let us then approach God's throne of grace with confidence, so that we may receive mercy and find grace to help us in our time of need (Hebrews 4:16).

REASONING OR CONTEXT

Some prayers of the petition include a brief explanation or context for the request. These appeals help to provide a deeper understanding of the circumstances. They also give insight into the circumstances behind the plea. Directions for their prayer sometimes require clarification.

I urge, then, first of all, that petitions, prayers, intercession, and thanksgiving be made for all people (1 Timothy 2:1).

HUMILITY AND SUBMISSION:

Often, individuals approach God humbly, recognizing their limitations by submitting to the Higher Power's will. While they make their requests, they acknowledge that the ultimate decision rests with the Father.

> *Humble yourselves before the Lord, and he will lift you up* (James 4:10).

GRATITUDE AND PRAISE:

Prayers of petition can also include expressions of gratitude and praise for the blessings and favors received from the Maker in the past.

> *Devote yourselves to prayer, being watchful and thankful* (Colossians 4:2).

CLOSING:

Prayers often conclude with a closing statement, reiterating the petitioner's trust and faith in the Creator and affirming their willingness to accept the outcome according to the wisdom of God.

Spiritual Application:

Prayers of petition identify only one type of prayer. Different forms of prayers serve various spiritual purposes. Many individuals find solace and a sense of connection through expressing their needs and desires to the Divine, believing that their petitions are heard and considered.

Lessons within the Lesson:

List the thought-provoking verses or statements that spoke to you in this chapter.

Which statement may have the utmost impact on your prayer life?

How will your prayer life change because of this statement?

List the steps you will take to make the changes necessary to strengthen your prayer life.

7: PRAYERS OF CONTRITION

1 John 1:5-7

Opening Prayer: (Today's prayer is adapted from Psalms 51:1-4).

Have mercy on me, O God, according to Your unfailing love. Hear me as I plead for Your great compassion. Blot out my transgressions. Wash away all my iniquity and cleanse me from my sin. For I know my transgressions and my sins are always before me. Against You and only You have I sinned and done what is evil in Your sight. You have proved Your righteousness when You speak. You, O Lord, are just and justified when You judge. Cleanse me and make me whole again. In Your Son's name, I pray. Amen!

Today's Bible Verse: 1 John 1:5-7.

This is the message we have heard from him and declare to you: God is light; in him there is no darkness at all. If we claim to have fellowship with him yet walk in the darkness, we lie and do not live by the truth. But if we walk in the light, as he is in the light, we have fellowship with one another, and the blood of Jesus, his Son, purifies us from all sin.

Associated Scriptures:

So I say, walk by the Spirit, and you will not gratify the desires of the flesh. For the flesh desires what is contrary to the Spirit, and the Spirit what is contrary to the flesh. They are in conflict with each other, so that you are not to do whatever you want. (Galatians 5:16-17).

Blessed is the one whose transgression is forgiven, whose sin is covered. Blessed is the man against whom the Lord counts no iniquity, and in his spirit there is no deceit (Psalm 32:1-5).

To some who were confident of their own righteousness and looked down on everybody else, Jesus told this parable: Two men went up to the temple to pray, one a Pharisee and the other a tax collector. The Pharisee stood up and prayed about himself: God, I thank you that I am not like other men — robbers, evildoers, adulterers or even like this tax collector. I fast twice a week and give a tenth of all I get. But the tax collector stood at a distance. He would not even look up to heaven, but beat his breast and said, God, have mercy on me, a sinner. I tell you that this man, rather than the other, went home justified before God. For everyone who exalts himself will be humbled, and he who humbles himself will be exalted (Luke 18:9-14).

Correlative Quotes:

John's point is that if Christians live in the light where God is, then there is mutual fellowship between Himself and them. That is, they have fellowship with Him and He has fellowship with them. The light itself is the fundamental reality which they share. Thus true communion with God is living in the sphere where one's experience is illumined by the truth of what God is. It is to live open to His revelation.[23] – Walvoord and Zuck

Darkness represents the self-sphere. Light represents the God-sphere. God is kin with everything clean, good, kind. Self spoils even good things by throwing upon them the shadow of its own darkness.[24] – Barlow

If we say that we have no sin. The preceding words had reminded St, John that even mature Christians, though

---

[23] John Walvoord and Roy B. Zuck, The Bible Knowledge Commentary, N. T., Ibid.

[24] George Barlow (Editor), A Preachers Complete Homiletical Commentary, Vol. XXX Public Domain, New York, Funk and Wagnalls Company, London and Toronto, 1896, P. 239.

certainly not *walking in darkness*, yet have sinful tendencies in themselves: sensuous impulses, non-spiritual inclinations, lack of self-knowledge, a lowered standard, principles and views borrowed partly from the world, wavering of will, and hence even graver faults. Not to admit this would be to mislead ourselves.[25] – Ellicott

Author's Notes:

INTRODUCTION

The prayer of regret means speaking directly to God's will by confessing our sins. When we are living in disobedience, we are out of the wheelhouse of the Almighty. We cannot make requests of the Lord when we find ourselves out of fellowship with the Spirit. We can ask God for anything at any time. However, He will only answer when we have a pure heart. Remorseful prayer, also known as the prayer of repentance, is a humble and sincere prayer in which an individual expresses remorse for their sins and seeks His forgiveness. It is a significant aspect of many religious traditions, including Christianity. The prayer of deliverance is an acknowledgment of shortcomings, a plea for mercy, and a desire to turn away from sinful behavior and live in alignment with God.

THE PRAYER OF CONTRITION

ADDRESSING GOD: (Matthew 6:9)

The prayer often begins by addressing God directly. This direct approach suggests titles like *Heavenly Father, God, Lord, or Merciful Savior.*

CONFESSION OF SINS: (1 John 1:9)

The individual confesses their specific sins to God. It is a genuine disclosure of the ways in which they have fallen short of His standard and the harm they may have caused to themselves and others.

SINCERE REMORSE: (Psalm 3:4)

Repentance expresses genuine sorrow and remorse for the sins committed. This sorrow stems from fear of punishment and an

---

[25] C. J. Ellicott, (Charles John), A New Testament Commentary for English Readers, 1819-1905. Public Domain, Published by E. D. Dolton and Company, New York, 1897, P. 475-6.

understanding of the offense to God and evokes a desire to change.

REQUEST FOR FORGIVENESS: (Psalm 25:11)

The person prays and asks for mercy and forgiveness. They seek release from the guilt and the burden of their sins. God is willing to pardon those who approach Him with a repentant heart.

COMMITMENT TO CHANGE: (Jeremiah 7:5-8)

A key element of the prayer of repentance is the sincere intention to change sinful ways and lead a more righteous life. The individual desires to repent for their disobedience and walk in God's ways..

TRUST IN GOD'S GRACE: (Psalm 13:5)

Remorse opens the door to the Lord's abundant grace and love. Those who repent believe His mercy, forgiveness, empowerment, transformation, and spiritual growth are possible through love.

SURRENDER TO GOD'S WILL: (1 Kings 5:18)

Finally, the prayer may end with an expression of surrender to His will, inviting God to guide the person's life and help them remain faithful to their commitment to change.

Spiritual Application:

The prayer of repentance is not just a ritualized act. It represents a deeply personal and spiritual encounter with God. It is an act of humility, vulnerability, and honesty before the divine, seeking reconciliation and restoration in the relationship with God. Through this form of prayer, individuals seek comfort, healing, and the strength to live in alignment with their faith and values.

Lessons within the Lesson:

List the thought-provoking verses or statements that spoke to you in this chapter.

Which statement may have the utmost impact on your prayer life?

How will your prayer life change because of this statement?

List the steps you will take to make the changes necessary to strengthen your prayer life.

8: PRAYERS OF FAITH

Matthew 21:21-22

Opening Prayer: (Today's prayer is adapted from Psalms 51:6-9.)

O Lord, my Savior, You desire truth from within the deepest reaches of my mind and heart. You teach me wisdom in the inmost place. I know Your truth, but obedience is difficult. Cleanse me with herbal washes, and I will be clean. Wash me with the blood of Jesus, and I will be whiter than snow. For it is Your Son's precious name, I pray. Amen!

Today's Bible Verse: **Matthew 21:21-22 (NKJV).**

So Jesus answered and said to them, Assuredly, I say to you, if you have faith and do not doubt, you will not only do what was done to the fig tree, but also if you say to this mountain, Be removed and be cast into the sea, it will be done. And whatever things you ask in prayer, believing, you will receive.

Associated Scriptures:

And without faith it is impossible to please Him, for whoever would draw near to God must believe that He exists and that He rewards those who seek Him (Hebrews 11:5, ESV).

So faith comes from hearing, and hearing through the word of Christ (Romans 10:17, ESV).

Now faith is the assurance of things hoped for, the conviction of things not seen (Hebrews 11:1, ESV).

Correlative Quotes:

> We ought not to tolerate for a minute the ghastly and grievous thought that God will not answer prayer. His nature, as manifested in Christ Jesus, demands it.[26] – Spurgeon

> The principle taught in the parable (the fig tree, Matthew 21:18-22) was that religious profession without spiritual reality is an abomination to God and is cursed.[27] – MacArthur

> Jesus used this event to teach a lesson in faith, for if they had genuine faith in God they not only would be able to do miracles such as cursing the tree (the fig tree, Matthew 21:18-22), but they would be able to move mountains.[28] – Walvoord and Zuck

Author's Notes:

INTRODUCTION: THE PRAYER OF FAITH:

The prayer of faith is a powerful and essential concept in the Bible, particularly in the New Testament. It is a prayer that expresses unwavering trust and confidence in God's ability to fulfill His promises and work in response to the believer's petitions. The prayer of faith is rooted in the belief that God is loving, all-powerful, and faithful to His Word and that He hears and responds to the prayers of His people.

We should always pray believing. God will answer. God is all powerful. Plus, He owns all things. In Isaiah 65:24, God says: *I will answer them (believers) before they even call to me. While they are still talking about their needs, I will go ahead and answer their prayers!* God answers prayer in three ways: Wait, Yes, No.

WAIT

Timing is everything with God. When God says yes, He means the best is yet to come. He says Be Patient. When we listen to Him and do not worry or frustrate over any unanswered request, God blesses our socks off. *But those who wait on the*

---

[26] Charles Spurgeon, The Golden Key of Prayer, Public Domain, March 12, 1865
   Scripture: Jeremiah 33:3From: Metropolitan Tabernacle Pulpit Volume 11.

[27] The MacArthur, New Testament Commentary, Moody Press and John MacArthur, Jr., Used by permission, Fair Use Authorization, Section 107, of the Copyright Law

[28] John Walvoord and Roy B. Zuck, The Bible Knowledge Commentary, N. T. Ibid.

LORD Shall renew their strength; They shall mount up with wings like eagles, They shall run and not be weary, They shall walk and not faint (Isaiah 40:31).

YES

Lord, give me patience and give it to me now. These words are the cry of impatience. Sit back, relax, and wait for the yes. When we ask in His name, believing we will receive our petition, God will say yes. *For no matter how many promises God has made, they are "Yes" in Christ. And so through him the "Amen" is spoken by us to the glory of God* (2 Corinthians 1:20).

NO

God will not give us everything we want. He determines the need. The decision is not with us. When the Creator says no, it is always for our best. We should not complain about it. King David prayed and fasted, requesting life for his son. When the boy died, David moved forward with his life. God said no. David accepted the answer graciously.

The primary biblical reference that directly addresses the prayer of faith is in James 5:15-16 (New Testament): *And the prayer offered in faith will make the sick person well; the Lord will raise them up. If they have sinned, they will be forgiven. Therefore, confess your sins to each other and pray for each other so that you may be healed. The prayer of a righteous person is powerful and effective*. This passage emphasizes the importance of both faith and righteousness in prayer. When a believer prays with genuine faith and trusts in God's goodness and sovereignty, there is a potential for healing and restoration physically and spiritually.

ELEMENTS OF FAITH IN PRAYER INCLUDE:

UNWAVERING TRUST:

The prayer of faith is characterized by unwavering trust and confidence in God's character and His promises. Believers approach God with the assurance that He hears and responds to their heartfelt prayers.

GOD'S WILL:

The prayer of faith seeks to align the petitioner's desires with God's will. While expressing specific requests, the believer acknowledges that

God's plans may differ from theirs and surrenders to His divine wisdom and sovereignty.

SUBMISSION:

The prayer of faith involves a humble and submissive attitude before God. It acknowledges human limitations and recognizes that ultimate control lies with God, not the person praying.

RIGHTEOUSNESS:

The passage in James emphasizes the effectiveness of the prayer of a righteous person. Righteousness here refers to a right relationship with God, achieved through faith in Jesus Christ and practicing obedience to His teachings.

EXPECTANCY:

The prayer of faith carries an expectancy that God will answer according to His perfect timing and wisdom. Believers trust that God's response will be for their ultimate good, even if it may not align with their immediate desires.

Spiritual Application:

It is important to note that the prayer of faith is not about a specific formula or ritual but about the condition of the heart and the depth of trust in God. Faith in prayer is not a guarantee that God will always answer in the way we desire, but it is a posture that acknowledges His sovereignty and leans on His wisdom and love in all circumstances.

Lessons within the Lesson:

List the thought-provoking verses or statements that spoke to you in this chapter.

Which statement may have the utmost impact on your prayer life?

How will your prayer life change because of this statement?

List the steps you will take to make the changes necessary to strengthen your prayer life.

9: PRAYERS OF ADORATION

Isaiah 6:1-3

Opening Prayer:

Dear God, I come before You today with a heart filled with awe and adoration. You are the Creator of the heavens and the earth. I am humbled by the vastness and beauty of Your creation. Your wisdom and understanding are beyond measure, and I marvel at the intricacies of Your design. Lord, You are worthy of all praise and honor. Your love is boundless and unfailing, and your grace is abundant. I am grateful for the countless blessings You have bestowed upon me and for the gift of life itself. You are the Alpha and the Omega, the beginning and the end. You are the Rock on which I stand, the Savior who redeemed me, and the Comforter who guides me. Your mercy and forgiveness are unending, and I thank You for your patience with me, even when I fall short. Your faithfulness is steadfast, and I am in awe of Your unchanging love. I lift my voice in adoration, singing praises to Your name. You are the King of kings and the Lord of lords, and I surrender my heart to You in worship. Thank You for Your presence in my life, hearing my prayers, and guiding my steps. I adore You, Lord, and I long to know You more deeply each day. In Jesus' name, I pray. Amen!

Today's Bible Verse: Isaiah 6:1-3.

In the year that King Uzziah died, I saw the Lord seated on a throne, high and exalted, and the train of his robe filled the temple. Above him were seraphs, each with six wings: With two wings they covered their faces, with two

49

they covered their feet, and with two they were flying. And they were calling to one another: Holy, holy, holy is the Lord Almighty; the whole earth is full of his glory.

Associated Scriptures:

I call to the Lord , who is worthy of praise, and I am saved from my enemies. The cords of death entangled me; the torrents of destruction overwhelmed me. The cords of the grave coiled around me; the snares of death confronted me. In my distress I called to the Lord; I cried to my God for help. From his temple he heard my voice; my cry came before him, into his ears (Psalms 18:3-6).

No one is like you, LORD; you are great, and your name is mighty in power (Jeremiah 10:6).

How abundant are the good things that you have stored up for those who fear you, that you bestow in the sight of all, on those who take refuge in you (Psalm 31:19).

Correlative Quotes:

Believers love Jesus with a deeper affection then they dare to give to any other being. They would sooner lose father and mother then part with Christ. They hold all earthly comforts with a loose hand, but they carry Him fast locked in their bosoms. They voluntarily deny themselves for His sake, but they are not to be driven to *deny* Him. It is scant love which the fire of persecution can dry up; the true believer's love is a deeper stream than this. Men have labored to divide the faithful from their Master, but their attempts have been fruitless in every age. Neither crowns of honor, now frowns of anger, have untied this more than Gordian knot. This is no every-day attachment which the world's power may at length dissolve. Neither man nor devil have found a key which opens this lock.[29] – Spurgeon

This threefold declaration of God's holiness is often taken as

---

[29] Charles Spurgeon, Morning Thought, August 7 a.m., Public Domain, heartlight.org/spurgeon/0807-am

an indication of the triune God in the Old Testament. Note in verse eight that one God speaks he uses the plural pronoun us. The Hebrew texts makes it clear that Isaiah saw the Lord (*Adonai*) sitting upon the throne and it was the Lord (Jehovah) whom the seraphim worship, substantiating that Jehovah and *Adonai* we're one and the same.[30] – Wemp

The threefold repetition of the word holy suggests supreme or complete holiness.[31] – Walvoord and Zuck

Author's Notes:

INTRODUCTION

A prayer of adoration is a type of prayer that focuses on praising and worshiping God for His greatness, goodness, and majesty. It is a form of invocation that expresses reverence, love, and admiration towards God, acknowledging His attributes and exalting His name.

This example of prayer typically begins by addressing God and acknowledging His presence and divine nature. It may include expressions of awe and wonder at God's power, creativity, and love. Prayers of adoration often involve using words of praise and affirmation. Quoting verses from the Bible, or singing hymns and songs of worship, praise God for who He is and what He has accomplished in us.

GOD IS WORTHY:

> *Great is the Lord , and most worthy of praise, in the city of our God, his holy mountain. For this God is our God for ever and ever; He will be our guide even to the end* (Psalms 48:1 and 14).

God is worthy. Revelation 4:1 says: *Worthy are You, our Lord and our God, to receive glory and honor and power; for You created all things, and because of Your will they existed, and were created..* He loves us (John 3:16). God created us (Genesis1:27).

---

[30] Sumner Wemp, Liberty Bible Commentary, published by Old Gospel Hour, Nashville, Tenn. P. 2501, Used by permission, Fair Use Authorization, Section 107, of the Copyright Law P. 1308-1309.

[31] John Walvoord and Roy Zuck, The Bible Knowledge Commentary, O. T. Victor Books, a division of SP Publications, Wheaton, Illinois 60187, P. 1045. Used by permission, Fair Use Authorization, Section 107, of the Copyright Law.

He loved us in spite of our sin. Romans 5:8 explains: *But God demonstrates his own love for us in this: While we were still sinners, Christ died for us.*

While we were at war with God, He gave us peace. John 14:27 says: *Peace I leave with you; my peace I give you. I do not give to you as the world gives. Do not let your hearts be troubled and do not be afraid.*

GOD'S GREATNESS:

For great is the LORD, and greatly to be praised; He also is to be feared above all gods (Psalm 96:4).

God's greatness refers to the immense and incomprehensible attributes, qualities, and characteristics making God supremely superior, majestic, and beyond human understanding. The concept of the Creator's greatness is a fundamental aspect of Christian beliefs. This characteristic describes the vastness and magnificence of His divine nature.

GOD'S GOODNESS:

The LORD is compassionate and gracious, slow to anger, abounding in love (Psalm 103:8).

God's goodness describes His inherent nature. His moral excellence, kindness, benevolence, and generosity reflect the Lord's goodness. A fundamental aspect of His existence, fairness has become a core attribute of His divinity. God's goodness illustrates His love and concern for humanity. His actions of love, interactions with creation, and overall character are fundament attributes.

GOD'S MAJESTY

Yours, LORD, is the greatness and the power and the glory and the majesty and the splendor, for everything in heaven and earth is yours. Yours, LORD, is the kingdom; you are exalted as head over all (1 Chronicles 29:11).

Throughout history, poets, artists, and thinkers have attempted to capture the essence of God's majesty through various mediums, whether through poetic verses, awe-inspiring artworks, or philosophical contemplations. However, the full range of God's splendor remains beyond the scope of human comprehension, inviting individuals to embrace the mystery and beauty of the divine. Look into the sky on a clear evening. Hold a newborn baby as it cuddles its head into your neck. Visit a waterfall in late Spring or a forest in the Fall. You will begin to understand the majestic nature of God. God is everywhere at the same time. Jeremiah 23:23-24 states: *Am I only a God nearby," declares the LORD, "and not a God far away? Who can hide in secret places so that I cannot see them?" declares the LORD. "Do not I fill heaven and earth?" declares the LORD.*

WE ARE NOT WORTHY:

> *Anyone who loves their father or mother more than me is not worthy of me; anyone who loves their son or daughter more than me is not worthy of me* (Matthew 10:37).

Interpreting this scripture can be complex. It addresses the tension between religious commitment and family obligations. Some theologians see Matthew 10:37 as a reminder that our relationship with God reaches beyond earthly attachments. Others interpret it as a call to ensure family relationships don't become idols overshadowing one's relationship with God.

OUR REVERENCE:

> *In the days of His flesh, He offered up both prayers and supplications with loud crying and tears to the One able to save Him from death, and He was heard because of His piety* (Hebrews 5:7).

Because of Christ's sacrifice, we now have full access to God (Ephesians 3:12). We connect to God through the Holy Spirit. This bond permits us to approach Him *boldly* without fear. Prayer allows us to connect (1 John 3:22).

OUR LOVE:

> *So take diligent heed to yourselves to love the Lord your God* (Joshua 23:11).

Our relationship with God centers on the Godhead. God's love created us. Christ's love died and rose again to establish a permanent relationship with humanity. The Spirit of God enters into our lives through salvation. All these actions find their root in God's great love for us. We must love to accept it and promote salvation to others (Matthew 28:18-20).

OUR ADMIRATION

Through Jesus, therefore, let us continually offer to God
a sacrifice of praise—the fruit of lips that openly profess
his name (Hebrews 13:15).

This verse in Hebrews encourages a consistent and ongoing practice of offering praise to God. This concept of continually praying to God parallels the Old Testament concept of offering physical sacrifices as acts of worship.

There must be some reality in prayer, it must be his intention to
hear and to answer prayer, or else he would not put it thus,
Men ought always to pray.[32] – Spurgeon

Spiritual Application:

In a prayer of adoration, the focus is on God, His attributes, and His works, rather than on personal requests or concerns. It is a way to express love and devotion to God and to grow in a deeper relationship with Him.

Lessons within the Lesson:

List the thought-provoking verses or statements that spoke to you in this chapter.

Which statement may have the utmost impact on your prayer life?

How will your prayer life change because of this statement?

List the steps you will take to make the changes necessary to strengthen your prayer life.

---

[32] Charles Spurgeon, When Should We Pray, Metropolitan Tabernacle Pulpit Volume 43, Public Domain, spurgeon.org/resource-library/sermons/when-should-we-pray/#flipbook/. No page numbers.

10: PRAYERS OF CONSECRATION OR DEDICATION

1 Corinthians 6:19-20

Opening Prayer: (The opening prayer is adapted from Psalms 51:15-19).

O Lord, open my lips, and my mouth will declare your praise. You no longer require blood sacrifices, or I would bring an offering to You. Offerings to You, O God, include a broken spirit, a remorseful attitude, and a repentant heart. You will not despise these tributes. In Your time and by Your resolve, make us prosper; build up the walls of our resistance to temptation. Then there will be righteous sacrifices to delight you. We will offer ourselves a personal offering. We will become wholly acceptable in Your sight. O Lord, you are our strength and redeemer. In the Lord's name, we pray. Amen!

Today's Bible Verse: 1 Corinthians 6:19-20.

Do you not know that your bodies are temples of the Holy Spirit, who is in you, whom you have received from God? You are not your own; you were bought at a price. Therefore honor God with your bodies.

Associated Scriptures:

Always give yourselves fully to the work of the Lord because you know that your labor in the Lord is not in vain (1 Corinthians 15:58).

So we make it our goal to please him, whether we are at home in the body or away from it. For we must all appear before the judgment seat of Christ, so that each of us may receive what is due us for the things done while in the body, whether good or bad (2 Corinthians 5:9-10).

Sing and make music from your heart to the Lord, always giving thanks to God the Father for everything, in the name of our Lord Jesus Christ (Ephesians 5:19-20).

Correlative Quotes:

Now, if it is true that we are not our own, and I hope it is true to many here present, then the inference from it is, "I have no right to injure myself in any way." My body is not my own; I have no right then, as a Christian, to do anything with it that would defile it. The apostle is mainly arguing against sins of the flesh, and he says, "The body is not for fornication, but for the Lord; and the Lord for the body." We have no right to commit uncleanness, because our bodies are the members of Christ, and not our own![33] – Spurgeon

God the Father created our bodies; God the Son redeemed them and made them part of His body; and God the Spirit indwells our bodies and makes them the very temple of God. How can we defile God's temple by using our bodies for immorality?[34] – Wiersbe

So Paul calls for sexual purity not only because of the way sexual sin affects the body, but because the body it affects is not even the believer's own. Understanding the reality of the phrase the Holy Spirit who is in you, whom you have from God should give us as much commitment to purity as any knowledge of divine truth could.[35] – MacArthur

Author's Notes:

---

[33] Charles Spurgeon, Bought With A Price, Sermon 1004, Public Domain, spurgeongems.org, P. 5.

[34] Warren Wiersbe, The Wiersbe Bible Commentary: New Testament, Ibid., P. 471.

[35] John MacArthur, The John MacArthur New Testament Commentary, 1 Corinthians, Moody Press, Chicago, Used by permission, Fair Use Authorization, Section 107, of the Copyright Law, P. 152.

INTRODUCTION

Prayers of consecration or dedication hold deep and spiritual significance. These prayers often set apart a person, place, object, or event for a specific purpose or divine service. They reflect the intention to sanctify and devote something to God for a greater purpose. Our dedication to Him is revealed in the way we follow God.

2 Peter 1:5-8 states: *Make every effort to add to your faith goodness; and to goodness, knowledge, and to knowledge, self-control; and to self-control, perseverance; and to perseverance, godliness, and to godliness, mutual affection; and to mutual affection, love. For if you possess these qualities in increasing measure, they will keep you from being ineffective and unproductive in your knowledge of our Lord Jesus Christ.*

Christianity uses these prayers to symbolize offering something to a Greater Power while seeking blessings, protection, and guidance. The words and rituals associated with consecration prayers vary widely. The underlying purpose includes reverence, humility, and a desire to address, and align with an Omnipotent Maker.

Consecration prayers address the object or entity being dedicated, but they also include the person or group making the dedication (1 Chronicles 26:20). They provide an opportunity for individuals or communities to express their commitment and faith, acknowledging their connection to the divine and their willingness to uphold the purpose for which the dedication is being performed (Hosea 6:1a, 2-3).

Our bodies are the temple of God. He lives in us and works through us to His honor and glory. We should dedicate and consecrate ourselves to Him daily. Blessings await those who trust in the Lord.

INTENT AND PURPOSE:

At the core of acknowledgment, we find the intention to set ourselves apart for something or someone. Our purpose should include service to God and include others. This attitude of service reflects the human desire to connect with their Maker and align with higher values.

SPIRITUAL CONNECTION:

Our alignment with God sets a spiritual anchor for our relationship with Him. It acknowledges the presence of a higher power and seeks its involvement, guidance, and approval. The language and imagery emphasize humility, reverence, and submission to the divine will.

TRANSCENDENCE OF THE ORDINARY:

Through dedication, ordinary moments seem to be elevated to a higher plane of existence. These experiences reflect the human aspiration to find meaning and significance in everyday life and to connect the temporal with the eternal creator.

COMMUNITY AND IDENTITY:

Prayer will also unify communities or groups under a shared purpose or belief. They reinforce the sense of belonging and identity among congregants by dedicating themselves to a common cause.

PERSONAL TRANSFORMATION:

These prayers can also symbolize internal transformations. Individuals might dedicate themselves to a life of service, self-improvement, or spiritual growth through a personal union with Jesus.

Spiritual Application:

Prayers of consecration or dedication are effectual expressions of human spirituality and devotion. They bridge the gap between the material and the spiritual worlds, providing a means to connect with God, express intention, and seek God's sanctification. We desire to dedicate these special people and objects to God.

Lessons within the Lesson:

List the thought-provoking verses or statements that spoke to you in this chapter.

Which statement may have the utmost impact on your prayer life?

How will your prayer life change because of this statement?

List the steps you will take to make the changes necessary to strengthen your prayer life.

11. PRAYERS OF INTERCESSION

1 Timothy 2:1

Opening Prayer: (Today's prayer is adapted from Hebrews 7:25)

O Lord, You reside with Your creation. You sit enthroned above all things (Isaiah 6:1-3) and yet You abide in all things (Colossians 1:17). Therefore, Your power will save completely those who come to God through You, Jesus. Because we know You live to intercede for humanity, we praise Your Holy name. In Your name, we pray. Amen!

Today's Bible Verse: 1 Timothy 2:1

I urge, then, first of all, that petitions, prayers, intercession, and thanksgiving be made for all people.

Associated Scriptures:

For I know that this will turn out for my deliverance through your prayers and the provision of the Spirit of Jesus Christ (Philippians 1:19, NASB).

Pray for the peace of Jerusalem: May they prosper who love you (Psalm 122:6, NASB).

With all prayer and petition pray at all times in the Spirit, and with this in view, be on the alert with all perseverance and petition for all the saints (Ephesians 6:18).

Correlative Quotes:

What Christian does not pray for the salvation of friends and loved ones who do not know the Lord? The issue in this passage, however, is broader than praying for those close to us. It calls us to prayer for the lost in general; on behalf of all men.[36] – MacArthur

This means we should pray for the unsaved and the saved, for people near us and people far away, for enemies as well as friends.[37] – Wiersbe

Not much weight should be placed on the presumed distinctions between requests, prayers, and intercession. The terms are more likely designed to build on one another for emphasis.[38] – Walvoord and Zuck

Author's Notes:

INTRODUCTION

Intercessory prayer allows individuals or groups to pray on behalf of others. While praying for these needs, intercessors seek positive outcomes or assistance for one another's well-being or concerns. The purpose of intercessory prayer is rooted in understanding how prayer, when issued through faith, will change the direction for those with health or other life anxieties. God answers prayers when belief becomes the motivator.

> *Then Jesus answered, "Woman, you have great faith! Your request is granted." And her daughter was healed from that very hour* (Matthew 15:28).

Seeking to help others through prayer becomes a way of expressing care, compassion, and solidarity with others. God commands us to pray for others believers and for those who need salvation (Romans 10:1).

> *And pray in the Spirit on all occasions with all kinds of prayers and requests. With this in mind, be alert and always keep on praying for all the saints* (Ephesians 6:18).

---

[36] John MacArthur, The John MacArthur New Testament Commentary, 1 Timothy, Moody Press, Chicago, Used by permission, Fair Use Authorization, Section 107, of the Copyright Law, P. 58.

[37] Warren Wiersbe, The Wiersbe Bible Commentary: New Testament,, Ibid., P. 752.

[38] John Walvoord and Roy B. Zuck, The Bible Knowledge Commentary, N. T. Victor Books, Whitby, Ontario, Canada, Bucks, England, Used by permission, Fair Use Authorization, Section 107, of the Copyright Law

PURPOSES FOR INTERCESSORY PRAYER

REQUESTING HELP AND SUPPORT:

For this reason, since the day we heard about you, we have not stopped praying for you (Colossians 1:9).

Intercessory prayer allows people to ask for help, guidance, healing, or protection for others who face challenges, difficulties, or suffering. It's a way of seeking Divine assistance to alleviate pain or burdens that others are experiencing.

EXPRESSING EMPATHY AND COMPASSION:

The prayer of a righteous person is powerful and effective (James 5:16).

Intercessory prayer is an expression of empathy and compassion, showing concern for the well-being of others. By praying for someone's desires, believers demonstrate their care and willingness to support those in need.

STRENGTHENING COMMUNITY BONDS:

Love your enemies and pray for those who persecute you (Matthew 5:44).

Intercessory prayer can strengthen the sense of community within religious groups. When people come together to pray for a common purpose, it fosters a sense of unity, shared values, and a commitment to helping each other. Pray for all those in distress.

SEEKING DIVINE INTERVENTION:

For he will deliver the needy who cry out, the afflicted who have no one to help (Psalm 72:12).

God's children believe in the power of prayer. They communicate with God incessantly. Intercessory prayer becomes the way to intervention by conforming to the will of God through His Spirit. These prayers invite blessings and positive changes into the lives of those we pray for.

PROMOTING HEALING AND WELL-BEING:

Hope does not disappoint, because the love of God has been poured out in our hearts by the Holy Spirit who was given to us (Romans 5:5).

Intercessory prayer uses prayer to cause healing, both physical and emotional. Believers seek Divine healing for ailments, illnesses, or emotional distress experienced by others. We have the hope and power of prayer contributing to their recovery.

The results of prayer for others foster gratitude to God and inspire hope for the future. These prayers can help others cultivate gratitude by experiencing its blessings and positive aspects. It can also strengthen their hope by believing in the potential for positive change and improvement through divine intervention.

Spiritual Application:

Those who practice intercessory prayer, complying with God's design, become a living testimony to others. When the recipients experience answers to prayer, they begin to feel more deeply about the needs of others. This results in selflessness and the interconnectedness of those who seek deeper interpersonal relationships. It allows them to put these values into action through prayerful intentions.

It is important to note that the efficacy and interpretation of intercessory prayer can vary among different religious and spiritual traditions. Some believe intercessory prayer directly impacts outcomes, while others view it as a way to align oneself with divine will and find solace and peace in uncertain situations.

Lessons within the Lesson:

List the thought-provoking verses or statements that spoke to you in this chapter.

Which statement may have the utmost impact on your prayer life?

How will your prayer life change because of this statement?

List the steps you will take to make the changes necessary to strengthen your prayer life.

12: PRAYERS OF SUPPLICATION

Ephesians 6:18

Opening Prayer:

O Lord, I seek Your boundless grace and wisdom. I humbly come before You with a heavy heart. Answer my hopes and desires. As I kneel in the quiet sanctuary of my soul, I offer this prayer of supplication, seeking Your guidance, strength, and blessings. You, who know the depths of my heart and every thought in my mind, I appeal to You to grant me the courage to face the challenges of this day. With love for You and others along with a grateful heart and mind, I ask for Your support and blessing in my life and work. In Your blessed Son's name, I pray. Amen!

Today's Bible Verse: Ephesians 6:18.

And pray in the Spirit on all occasions with all kinds of prayers and requests. With this in mind, be alert and always keep on praying for all the Lord's people.

Associated Scriptures:

May these words of my mouth and this meditation of my heart be pleasing in your sight, LORD, my Rock and my Redeemer (Psalm 19:14).

Then hear in heaven their prayer and their supplication, and maintain their cause (1 Kings 8:45, NASB).

Deliver me according to your promise (Psalm 119:170).

The Lord has heard my supplication, The Lord receives my prayer (Psalm 6:9).

Correlative Quotes

Prayer crowns all lawful efforts with success and gives a victory when nothing else would.[39] – Barnes

Always be in communion with the Lord. Keep the receiver off the hook! Never have to say when you pray, *Lord, we come into Your presence*, because you never left His presence! A Christian must "pray always" because he is always subject to temptations and attacks of the devil. A surprise attack has defeated more than one believer who forgot to "pray without ceasing."[40] – Wiersbe

In every season: implying opportunity and exigency (*necessity, requirement, or circumstance*): the mind being always ready for prayer.[41] – Jamieson, Fausset, and Brown

Author's Notes:

INTRODUCTION

The prayer of supplication, as described in the Bible (Psalm 141: Hear my prayer O, Lord.), is a form of appeal where Christians and unbelievers humbly and earnestly ask God for specific needs, desires, or assistance. God only hears and answers the prayers of His children. In the old testament, God's plan for prayer appears in Proverbs 15:29: *The LORD is far from the wicked, but he hears the prayer of the righteous.*

In the New Testament, we see this truth mentioned in John 9:31: *We know that God does not listen to sinners. He listens to the godly person who does his will.*

Prayers of supplication come from deep in the soul of humanity and require great humility. Dependence on God's mercy and acknowledgment of human limitations exemplify these urgent prayers. These requests contain the recognition of God's sovereignty.

---

[39] Albert Barnes, Notes Explanatory and Practical, Public Domain, Blackie and Son, Queen Street, Glasgow, South College Street, Edinburgh, and Warwick Square, London, 1845, Free Download, Archive.org, P. 3495.

[40] Warren Wiersbe, The Wiersbe Bible Commentary: New Testament, Ibid. P. 624.

[41] Robert Jamieson, A.R. Fausset, David Brown, Commentary Critical and Explanatory on the Whole Bible, Public Domain, Copy Freely, Ibid., P. 358.

In the Bible, there are numerous examples of supplication prayers. The Book of Psalms, a collection of poetic prayers and hymns, contains the most well-known examples of this type of prayer.

Psalm 86:6-7 (NIV) is an example of a supplication prayer:

Hear my prayer, Lord; listen to my cry for mercy. When I am in distress, I call to you, because you answer me.

Another example found in the New Testament is in the book of Philippians. Philippians 4:6-7 (NIV) emphasizes the importance of bringing our requests to God through supplication and thanksgiving.

The prayer of supplication is a way for believers to express their heartfelt needs, concerns, and desires to God. It reflects a deep trust in God's providence and an understanding that God is not only a powerful deity but also a loving and caring Father who listens to the cries of His children.

This form of prayer encourages believers to approach God with humility, sincerity, and a recognition of their dependence on Him for all aspects of life.

Spiritual Application:

All the while that we are fighting in the girdle of truth, the breastplate of righteousness, the shoes of the gospel of peace, the shield of faith, the helmet or salvation, and the sword of the Spirit, we are to be in prayer.

Prayer is the very spiritual air that the soldier of Christ breathes. It is the all–pervasive strategy in which warfare is fought. Ephesians begins by lifting us up to the heavenlies and ends by pulling us down to our knees.[42] – MacArthur

Ultimately, supplication prayers in the Bible emphasize the importance of communication with God and seeking His guidance, support, and provision in all circumstances. We have the opportunity to be bold in asking God.

---

[42] John MacArthur, The John MacArthur New Testament Commentary, Ephesians, Moody Press, Chicago, Ill, preceptaustin.org/ephesians_618-20., Used by permission, Fair Use Authorization, Section 107, of the Copyright Law.

Boldness must always be tempered with humility. However, God is understanding, and He knows our motives. The mind of humanity is an open book to God. We cannot hide our thoughts and intent from Him. Our Creator is omniscient.

GOD SAID:

> *Do not pray for this people or offer any plea or petition for them, because I will not listen when they call to me in the time of their distress* (Jeremiah 11:14)

JEREMIAH PRAYED:

> *Do any of the worthless idols of the nations bring rain? Do the skies themselves send down showers? No, it is you, LORD our God. Therefore, our hope is in you, for you are the one who does all this* (Jeremiah 14:22).

This is an instance of amazing yet holy boldness. The prophet had received from the Lord the explicit command, *Do not pray for this people or offer any plea or petition for them* and yet, after expostulation with God, his heart grew so warm with sacred fervor, and his spirit became fired with such a passionate zeal, that he could not help pleading for the sinful nation. He poured out his soul in the vehement prayer and said to the Lord, *We will wait upon thee.*[43] – Spurgeon

Lessons within the Lesson:

List the thought-provoking verses or statements that spoke to you in this chapter.

Which statement may have the utmost impact on your prayer life?

How will your prayer life change because of this statement?

List the steps you will take to make the changes necessary to strengthen your prayer life.

---

[43] Charles Spurgeon, Intercession and Supplication, Sermon #2735, Public Domain, spurgeongems.org, P. 1.

13: A COMMONSENSE APPROACH TO PRAYER

Matthew 7:7-8

Opening Prayer:

Our Lord and Our God, You have promised in Matthew 6:33: *"But seek first his kingdom and his righteousness, and all these things will be given to you as well."* Therefore, Lord Jesus, I will glorify You and You only since I know You always keep Your Word. Your name is Holy! You are Holy, Holy, Holy. I will seek You, Lord, continually. My heart will rejoice in Your abundance. Your grace is overwhelming. Your love is reassuring. Great is Your faithfulness, O Lord. It is in Jesus' name we pray. Amen!

Today's Bible Verse: Matthew 7:7-8.

Ask and it will be given to you; seek and you will find; knock and the door will be opened to you. For everyone who asks receives; he who seeks finds; and to him who knocks, the door will be opened (Matthew 7:7-8).

Associated Scriptures:

If you, then, though you are evil, know how to give good gifts to your children, how much more will your Father in heaven give good gifts to those who ask him! (Matthew 7:11-12).

Again, I tell you that if two of you on earth agree about anything you ask for, it will be done for you by my Father in heaven. For where two or three come together in my name, there am I with them (Matthew 18:19-20).

And when you stand praying, if you hold anything against anyone, forgive him, so that your Father in heaven may forgive you your sins (Mark 11:25).

Correlative Quotes:

What is a door meant for if it is always to be kept shut? His doors are meant to open. They were made on purpose for entrance; and so the blessed gospel of God is made on purpose for you to enter into life and peace. It would be of no use to knock at a wall, but you may wisely knock at a door, for it is arranged for opening.[44] – Spurgeon

No soul can pray in vain that prays as directed above. The truth and faithfulness of the Lord Jesus are pledged for its success.- Ye SHALL receive – ye SHALL find – it SHALL be opened. These words are as strongly binding on the side of God, as thou shalt do no murder is on the side of man. Bring Christ's word, and Christ's sacrifice with thee, and not one of Heaven's blessings can be denied thee.[45] – Clarke

The three imperatives ask, seek, knock or, in the original, in the present tense suggesting both perseverance and frequent prayer. In the English language the first letter of each word forms an acrostic A-S-K. Fervent and continual prayer is to be made on behalf of those for whom we are concerned. God promises to answer every genuine prayer. Everything that we need for spiritual success has been promised.[46] – Hindson

Author's Notes:

INTRODUCTION

Intelligence and an extensive vocabulary alone will not replace common sense. Acquisition of knowledge, its application, and the ability to express it adequately are all essential for wisdom. Intuition may be the key

---

[44] Charles Spurgeon, Knock, #1743, Spurgeongems.org, Public Domain, P.4-5.

[45] Adam Clarke, by Samuel Dunn, The Gospel Harmonized with Notes, Explanatory, Experimental, and Practical, Printed for Thomas Tegg and Son, Dublin, P. 122.

[46] Edward E. Hindson, Liberty Bible Commentary, published by Old Gospel Hour, Nashville, Tenn. P. 2501, Used by permission, Fair Use Authorization, Section 107, of the Copyright Law, P. 1901.

to enlightenment, but only when it measures the holiness of God. Common sense is a work of the Holy Spirit. He will provide all these capabilities (Matthew 7:7-8, James 1:5). Developing a commonsense approach to praying involves approaching prayer with practicality, sincerity, and understanding. Its purpose and effects should be utmost in the believer's mind. Prayer involves an intimate connection with the Holy Spirit and His power. However, this statement doesn't necessarily exclude a rational and logical perspective. Common sense would tell us: Don't overthink the process.

SINCERITY AND AUTHENTICITY: Matthew 6:5.

A rational approach to prayer emphasizes genuine sincerity. It's about being honest with yourself and the divine entity you're praying to. Express your true feelings, hopes, and concerns without pretense. Sincere communication fosters a deeper connection and understanding.

CLARITY OF INTENT: 1 Corinthians 14:33.

Instead of relying solely on flowery language or complex requests, a realistic approach encourages clarity in expressing your desires and needs. Clearly stating what you're seeking in your prayers helps you focus your thoughts and intentions.

MINDFULNESS AND REFLECTION: 2 Timothy 2:7.

Taking a reasonable approach to prayer involves being mindful and reflective. Take the time to consider your thoughts and feelings and how they relate to your life and the world around you. This mindfulness can lead to insights and a better understanding of your situation.

PROBLEM SOLVING: Psalm 61:1-4.

Prayer can also be a way of seeking guidance concerning challenges in life. Taking a reasoned approach means using prayer as a tool for problem-solving. It's about seeking inspiration, wisdom, and ideas to navigate difficulties and make informed decisions.

ACTION AND EFFORT:

Prayer is imperative. This approach acknowledges taking practical action. Prayer can provide motivation, clarity, and emotional support, but it's often paired with efforts to achieve your goals. Recognizing that prayer can empower you will allow positive steps toward a goal.

GRATITUDE AND REFLECTION: 1 Thessalonians 5:18.

Common sense tells us to express gratitude for the positive aspects of our life. Reflecting on thankfulness can enhance your perspective and lead to a more positive mindset.

BALANCING FAITH AND REASON: Matthew 21:22.

We must not exclude faith. Faith brings a balance to logic. Acknowledging the spiritual dimension of prayer while also considering the practical implications is a win-win situation.

Not all prayers are answered immediately or in the way you expect. Patience and acceptance of the outcome, whether it aligns with your desires or not, are essential components of this approach.

COMMUNITY AND CONNECTION: Colossians 3:13.

Praying with others and seeking support from a community can enhance the logical approach to prayer. Sharing experiences, insights, and support can provide a well-rounded perspective on your concerns.

Spiritual Application:

In summary, an informed approach to prayer combines spiritual connection between the power of the Holy Spirit and our practicality. It involves sincerity, clarity, mindfulness, problem-solving, action, gratitude, and a balanced perspective. This approach recognizes that an individual's prayer is an intensely personal experience.

Lessons within the Lesson:

List the thought-provoking verses or statements that spoke to you in this chapter.

Which statement may have the utmost impact on your prayer life?

How will your prayer life change because of this statement?

List the steps you will take to make the changes necessary to strengthen your prayer life.

14. PRAYERS OF THANKSGIVING

Colossians 3:15

Opening Prayer: (Today's prayer is adapted from Psalm 95:1-7).

I will sing to You my Lord! I will shout joyfully to the Rock of my salvation. I will come before Your presence with thanksgiving. I shout joyfully to You with psalms. For You, my God, continue to stand as God alone. Your hands touch the deep places of the earth; the heights of the hills belong to You. The sea is Yours since You made it. Your hands formed the dry land. I worship and bow down; I kneel before the Lord my Maker. For You are my God, and I am Yours and Yours alone. There is no other God. In Your name, I pray. Amen!

Today's Bible Verse: **Colossians 3:15.**

Let the peace of Christ rule in your hearts, since as members of one body you were called to peace. And be thankful.

Associated Scriptures:

I will give to the Lord the thanks due to his righteousness, and I will sing praise to the name of the Lord, the Most High (Psalm 7:17).

I will give thanks to you, LORD, with all my heart; I will tell of all your wonderful deeds (Psalm 9:1).

Oh give thanks to the Lord, for he is good, for his steadfast love endures forever! (Psalm 107:1)

Correlative Quotes:

When there is peace in the heart, there will be praise on the lips: "And be ye thankful" (Colossians 3:15). The Christian out of God's will is never found giving sincere praise to God. When David covered up his sins, he lost his peace and his praise (Psalms 32; 51). When he confessed his sins, then his song returned.[47] – Wiersbe

An attitude of gratitude contributes to an enjoyment of spiritual tranquility, whereas grumbling makes for inner agitation[48] – Walvoord and Zuck.

Be thankful for your *calling*. Thanksgiving is prominent in Paul: forty-one times he uses the word. Not to have *peace ruling in your heart* would be inconsistent with the *calling in one body* and would be practical thanklessness to God who called us (Ephesians 5:4,19-20).[49] – Jamieson, Fausset, Brown

Author's Notes:

INTRODUCTION

Prayers of thanksgiving to God (Psalm 100:4), in Jesus' name (John 14:13-14), through the Spirit (Jude 1:20) are a fundamental aspect of Christianity. These prayers express gratitude for the blessings, provisions, and gifts believers know will come only from God. The opportunity for His children to acknowledge and appreciate the goodness of God in their lives stands alone as a reward enough.

GRATITUDE

> *I will pray with the spirit, and I will pray with understanding also: I will sing with the spirit, and I will sing with understanding also* (1 Corinthians 14:15).

Prayers of thanksgiving are expressions of gratitude to God. He is Lord. He created us. Prayers of gratitude allow followers of Christ to recognize and give thanks for all the blessings of the Creator. Whether

---

[47] Warren Wiersbe, The Wiersbe Bible Commentary: N. T., Ibid., P. 687.

[48] John Walvoord and Roy B. Zuck, The Bible Knowledge Commentary, Ibid.

[49] Robert Jamieson, A.R. Fausset, David Brown, Commentary Critical and Explanatory on the Whole Bible, N. T., Vol. II, P. 381.

these gifts are tangible (such as health, provision, or relationships) or intangible such as love, peace, and spiritual growth, we have an attitude of thankfulness.

HUMILITY:

> Seek the Lord , all you humble of the land, you who do what he commands. Seek righteousness, seek humility; perhaps you will be sheltered on the day of the Lord 's anger (Zephaniah 2:3).

Praying with humility acknowledges the good things in life. These answers to our requests are ultimately gifts from God. They help disciples recognize their lack of self-sufficiency while they depend on the grace and kindness of a higher power, their God and Father.

CONTENTMENT:

> And God is able to bless you abundantly, so that in all things at all times, having all that you need, you will abound in every good work (2 Corinthians 9:8).

Prayers of thanksgiving will lead to a sense of contentment and satisfaction. By acknowledging the goodness of Jesus in our lives, followers of Christ will not dwell on what they lack but will more likely find joy in what they have. Praise the Lord for the security we enjoy in Him.

CONNECTION WITH GOD:

> We give thanks to you, Lord God Almighty, who is and who was, for you have taken your great power and begun to reign (Revelation 11:17).

We desire a deeper connection with God. By expressing gratitude, the saved strengthen their relationship with their Maker. Recognizing God is actively involved in their lives connects us to His Power.

COMMUNITY AND SHARING:

> O magnify the Lord with me and let us exalt His name together (Psalm 34:3).

Prayers of thanksgiving shared in group worship allow believers to come together in gratitude. Sharing blessings and celebrating God's goodness as a community will strengthen bonds among believers.

FRAMING CHALLENGES:

> *But if we walk in the light, as he is in the light, we have fellowship with one another, and the blood of Jesus, his Son, purifies us from all sin* (1 John 1:7).

Prayers of thanksgiving also allow individuals to frame challenges and difficulties in a positive light. They focus on the lessons learned, the strength gained, and the growth initiated by facing adversity. When we walk in the light of His radiance, we experience His love.

CONSISTENT PRACTICE:

> *I thank Christ Jesus our Lord, who has given me strength, that He considered me faithful, appointing me to his service. Even though I was once a blasphemer and a persecutor, and a violent man, I was shown mercy because I acted in ignorance and unbelief. The grace of our Lord was poured out on me abundantly, along with the faith and love that are in Christ Jesus* (1 Timothy 1:12-14).

Incorporating prayers of thanksgiving into daily or regular spiritual practices help His children maintain a thankful and appreciative mindset.

Spiritual Application:

Whether through formal prayers, informal conversations with God, or even moments of silent reflection, prayers of thanksgiving provide an opportunity for individuals to express their heartfelt appreciation for the blessings they receive from God.

Lessons within the Lesson:

List the thought-provoking verses or statements that spoke to you in this chapter.

Which statement may have the utmost impact on your prayer life?

How will your prayer life change because of this statement?

List the steps you will take to make the changes necessary to strengthen your prayer life.

15: QUESTION #2: WHY DO WE PRAY?

Luke 18:1

Opening Prayer: (Todays prayer is adapted from Psalm 143:1-4, 7).

O Lord, hear my prayer. Listen to my cry for mercy. In Your faithfulness and righteousness, come to my relief. Do not judge Your servant alone since no one living is righteous before You. Evil people tempt me and would ruin my testimony. Unbelievers tempt me to sin. When I submit, disloyalty rears its ugly head. My spirit grows faint within me; my heart withers within me. Answer me quickly, O Lord, for my strength fails me. In Your complete and holy name. Amen!

Today's Bible Verse: **Luke 18:1 (NIV, NKJV).**

Then Jesus told his disciples a parable to show them that they should always pray and not give up (NIV).

Then He spoke a parable to them, that men always ought to pray and not lose heart (NKJV).

Associated Scriptures:

Watch and pray so that you will not fall into temptation. The spirit is willing, but the flesh is weak (Matthew 26:41).

Be joyful in hope, patient in affliction, faithful in prayer. (Romans 12:12).

Therefore, I tell you, whatever you ask for in prayer, believe that you have received it, and it will be yours (Mark 12:24).

Correlative Quotes:

> Christian prayer, then, shared a simple belief that God could be petitioned to intervene and effect changes in nature and in the course of world events. The immediate source of this confidence came from the teachings and examples of Jesus himself, such as the model prayer he offered (Matthew 6:9-13, Luke 11;2-4) and his assurance that one had only to ask the Father in order to receive what was needed (Matthew 7:7, Luke 11:9).[50] – Harrison, Bromeley, Henry

> Prayer is much more than the words of our lips; it is the desires of our hearts, *and our hearts are constantly "desiring" before Him,* even if we never speak a word. So, to "pray without ceasing" means to have such holy desires in our hearts, in the will of God, that we are constantly in loving communion with the Father, petitioning Him for His blessing.[51] -Wiersbe

> This is opposed to them, who pray not at all, or have left off prayer before God, or who pray only in distress; and suggests, that a man should pray as often as he has an opportunity; should be constant and assiduous at the throne of grace, and continue putting up his requests to God, though he does not presently return an answer[52] – Gill

Author's Notes:

INTRODUCTION

Prayer is simple. It is talking with God. Why we pray is more complicated. However, we pray for two reasons. The most common form of prayer is the request (John 16:24). The second method of talking with our Lord involves giving thanks or gratitude (Psalm 136:1). People may pray to God for diverse reasons, influenced by their beliefs, culture, and personal experiences. However, all prayers fall into these two categories: needs and thanksgiving.

---

[50] Bakers Dictionary of Theology, Everett Falconer Harrison, G. W. Bromeley, Carl F. H. Henry,
[51] Warren Wiersbe, The Wiersbe Bible Commentary: N. T. Ibid., P. 199.
[52] John Gill, John Gill's Exposition of the Entire Bible, 1810, Public Domain, Mathews & Leigh, London. P. 1892.

GOD'S WORD DEMANDS US TO PRAY

No specific verse exists saying God commands us to pray. Several passages in the Bible strongly encourage and emphasize the importance of prayer as an essential part of the relationship between humans and God.

GOD REQUIRES A SPIRITUAL CONNECTION:

Many pray frequently, hoping to connect with the Divine source of prayer. These seekers desire a deeper spiritual relationship with God. Prayer can provide a sense of closeness, comfort, and guidance in their spiritual journey.

GOD EXPECTS GRATITUDE:

Expressing gratitude is a common reason for prayer. People thank God for blessings, good health, happiness, and other positive results. God expects thankfulness. He doesn't just suggest it.

GOD WANTS BELIEVERS TO SEEK GUIDANCE:

Prayer can be a way to seek guidance, wisdom, and clarity in times of uncertainty. People may pray for direction in making important decisions or navigating challenging situations.

GOD STIMULATES CONFESSION AND FORGIVENESS:

Many religious traditions encourage prayer as a means of confessing sins or mistakes and seeking forgiveness from God. It's a way to acknowledge one's imperfections and to strive for spiritual growth.

REQUESTING HELP:

People often pray when they're facing difficulties, whether physical, emotional, or relational. They may seek help from God in overcoming obstacles, finding strength, or healing.

PROTECTION:

Prayer can be a way to ask for protection for oneself, loved ones, and the world. It's a way of seeking comfort and safety in an unpredictable world.

Comfort is sought by so many and received by few.

COMMUNITY AND UNITY:

Prayer can bring communities together, fostering a sense of unity and shared purpose. Group prayers can strengthen bonds among individuals who share common beliefs.

EXPRESSION OF FAITH:

For many, prayer is a fundamental expression of their faith. It reaffirms their belief in God and serves as a means of worship and devotion.

REFLECTION AND MEDITATION:

Prayer can provide a space for self-reflection and meditation. It allows individuals to pause, contemplate, and connect with their inner selves.

EXPRESSING LOVE:

People may pray to express their love for God. Just as we expect love from our family and friends, prayer is a way to express love and devotion to the Divine Father.

Spiritual Application:

It's important to note that the reasons for prayer vary greatly based on needs and individual experiences. Some may see prayer as a formal communication with their creator. Others envision a personal dialogue with God. They are both right. We pray to glorify our Maker. We also talk with Him about emergencies as well as long-term issues. Ultimately, the reasons for praying to God are deeply personal and can evolve as individuals travel their spirit-led journeys.

Lessons within the Lesson:

List the thought-provoking verses or statements that spoke to you in this chapter.

Which statement may have the utmost impact on your prayer life?

How will your prayer life change because of this statement?

List the steps you will take to make the changes necessary to strengthen your prayer life.

16: PRAYING IN THE WILL OF GOD

Luke 11:9-13

Opening Prayer:

O Lord, You are the maker of all things and the judge of all humanity. You make it rain in times of drought. You heal the sick when all seems hopeless. All life is in Your wondrous hands. I come before You with a heart open to Your will. Your wisdom surpasses all understanding. I humbly surrender my desires, plans, and intentions to Your sovereign hands. Lord, guide my steps along the path that aligns with Your perfect will. May Your Word be a lamp to my feet and a light to my path. Illuminate the way You have ordained for me. As I seek Your guidance, grant me discernment to recognize the doors You open and the ones You close. In this moment of prayer, I lift my hopes and dreams to You, knowing You see the bigger picture. If my requests align with Your plans, I ask for Your favor to bring them to fruition. But if my desires diverge from Your purpose, I trust You to redirect my path and replace my desires with Yours. In Jesus' name, I pray. Amen!

Today's Bible Verse: Luke 11:9-13.

So I say to you: Ask and it will be given to you; seek and you will find; knock and the door will be opened to you. For everyone who asks receives; the one who seeks finds; and to the one who knocks, the door will be opened. Which of you fathers, if your son asks for a fish, will give him a snake instead? Or if he asks for an egg, will give him a scorpion? If you then, though you are evil, know how to give good gifts to your children, how much more will your Father in heaven give the Holy Spirit to those who ask him!

Associated Scriptures:

Hezekiah turned his face to the wall and prayed to the Lord , Remember, O Lord , how I have walked before you faithfully and with wholehearted devotion and have done what is good in your eyes. And Hezekiah wept bitterly. Before Isaiah had left the middle court, the word of the Lord came to him: Go back and tell Hezekiah, the leader of my people, This is what the Lord , the God of your father David, says: I have heard your prayer and seen your tears; I will heal you. On the third day from now you will go up to the temple of the Lord. I will add fifteen years to your life (2 Kings 20:2-6).

Sacrifice thank offerings to God, fulfill your vows to the Most High, and call upon me in the day of trouble; I will deliver you, and you will honor me (Psalms 50:14-15).

On the day the Lord gave the Amorites over to Israel, Joshua said to the Lord in the presence of Israel: O sun, stand still over Gibeon, O moon, over the Valley of Aijalon. The sun stopped in the middle of the sky and delayed going down about a full day. There has never been a day like it before or since, a day when the Lord listened to a man (Joshua 10:12-14).

Correlative Quotes:

Hezekiah was quick to pray as he appealed to his faithful performance. A perfect heart does not mean it was perfect, but he served God wholeheartedly.[53] – Hartman

The sacrifices that the Lord commanded were indeed important to the spiritual life of the nation, but they did no good to the worshippers unless there was faith in the heart and a

---

[53] Harvey D. Hartman, 2 Kings, Liberty Bible Commentary, published by Old Gospel Hour, Nashville, Tenn. P. 2501, Used by permission, Fair Use Authorization, Section 107, of the Copyright Law, P. 736.

desire to honor the Lord. The animals they brought belonged to Him long before the worshipers ever saw them![54] – Wiersbe

It was noon and the hot sun was directly overhead when Joshua uttered this prayer. The moon was on the horizon to the west. The petition was quickly answered by the Lord. Joshua prayed in faith, and a great miracle resulted.[55]   – Walvoord and Zuck

Author's Notes:

INTRODUCTION

Praying in the will of God is a fundamental aspect of Christian prayer, reflecting the desire to align our petitions with God's plans and purposes. When we pray in God's will, we seek His guidance, acknowledge His sovereignty, and trust that He knows what is best for us and the world.

Understanding the will of God for humanity and concern for individual Christ followers is critical to the study of prayer. The Will of God is generally refers truth that there is a divine plan, purpose, or intention for humanity and that individuals should strive to align their actions and lives with this divine plan. The specifics of what this will entail can vary based on religious teachings, cultural contexts, and personal interpretations.

SPIRITUAL BELIEFS:

The will of God is often outlined in the scriptures, teachings, and traditions of other religions. For example, in Christianity, it's believed that God's will is revealed in the Bible, and individuals are encouraged to follow the commandments, the teachings of Jesus, and the overall message of love, compassion, and righteousness. Similarly, in Islam, the Quran and the teachings of the Prophet Muhammad outline the will of Allah.

---

[54] Warren Wiersbe, The Wiersbe Bible Commentary: O. T., bethelchurchmuncie.files. wordpress.com/2020/07/wiersbe-commentary-new-testament.pdf, Used by permission, Fair Use Authorization, Section 107, of the Copyright Law.

[55] John Walvoord and Roy B. Zuck, The Bible Knowledge Commentary, O. T. Victor Books, Whitby, Ontario, Canada, Bucks, England, Used by permission, Fair Use Authorization, Section 107, of the Copyright Law, P. 350.

MORALITY AND ETHICS:

Many belief systems emphasize living a moral and ethical life as a part of God's will. They believe actions like treating others with kindness, honesty, and fairness, and striving to make positive contributions to society will lead to eternal life.

However, a lifestyle of honesty and integrity will not provide eternal life. Eternal life comes only through belief in Jesus Christ (Ephesians 2:8-9 and Romans 10:9-10).

PURPOSE AND CALLING:

Some individuals believe that God has a specific purpose or calling for each person, and they seek to discover and fulfill that purpose in their lives. This belief could involve using one's talents, passions, and abilities to serve others, making the world better. The combinations are endless.

PRAYER AND GUIDANCE:

Believers seek guidance from God through prayer. They may ask for wisdom and clarity to understand and follow the divine will. *Until now you have not asked for anything in my name. Ask and you will receive, and your joy will be complete* (John 16:24).

SUFFERING AND CHALLENGES:

Believers may see challenges and suffering as a part of God's plan for personal growth, learning, and testing of faith. This perspective can help individuals find meaning and strength in difficult times.

We find comfort in knowing God will help us through difficult times when we ask. Romans 15:13 gives us joy when it says: *May the God of hope fill you with all joy and peace as you trust in him, so that you may overflow with hope by the power of the Holy Spirit.*

FREE WILL AND CHOICES:

You, my brothers and sisters, were called to be free. But do not use your freedom to indulge the flesh ; rather, serve one another humbly in love (Galatians 5:13).

The concept of free will adds complexity to God's will. Many belief systems assert that humans have the freedom to make choices, and these choices can either align with or deviate from God's will. Striking a balance

82

between divine sovereignty and human agency is a topic of philosophical and theological discussion.

Spiritual Application:

INTERPRETATION AND DIVERSITY:

It's important to note that interpretations of the will of God can vary widely within and between religious traditions. Different individuals and communities may have different understandings of what it means to follow God's will.

Ultimately, the will of God is a personal and spiritual concept, and individuals may find meaning, purpose, and guidance through their beliefs and practices as they seek to live in harmony with what they perceive as divine intention.

Praying in the will of God is a fundamental aspect of Christian prayer, reflecting the desire to align our petitions with God's plans and purposes. When we pray in God's will, we seek His guidance, acknowledge His sovereignty, and trust Him to know what is best for us and the world. Here's a brief guide on praying in the will of God.

SEEK GOD'S HEART

Before praying, seek God's heart through Scripture, meditation, and reflection. The Bible is a rich source of wisdom. Scripture reveals God's character, values, and desires. As you read and study His word, you will gain insight into what aligns with God's will.

SURRENDER

Approach prayer with a heart of surrender. Jesus demonstrated this in the Garden of Gethsemane when He prayed: *Not my will, but yours be done (Luke 22:42)*. A humble attitude acknowledges that God's plans are higher and wiser than ours. Yield your desires and intentions to God, allowing Him to shape your prayers.

PRAY IN ALIGNMENT WITH SCRIPTURE

Praying in God's will often involves praying by the principles and promises found in the Bible. God's Word serves as a guide for our prayers. When our prayers are rooted in Scripture, we have confidence we are praying in line with His purposes.

LISTEN AND WAIT

Prayer is a two-way conversation. As you pray, spend time listening to God's leading and guidance. God may speak to your heart through His Spirit, confirming His will and guiding your prayers.

TRUST GOD'S TIMING:

God's timing is perfect. However, it doesn't always match our expectations. While you may have specific requests, trust God, He knows the ideal time for answers. Patience represents the elementary aspect of praying in God's will.

BE OPEN TO HIS RESPONSE

Praying in the will of God means being open to His response, whether it's "yes," "no," or "wait." God answers our prayers based on His wisdom and love for us. If He closes one door, it's because He has something better in store.

PRIORITIZE GOD'S GLORY

Ultimately, praying in the will of God should prioritize His glory and the advancement of His Kingdom. Ask yourself how your prayers align with God's desire to bring about His purposes in the world and in the lives of all people (John 3:16).

Remember that God loves you and desires a relationship with you. As you seek His will in prayer, trust that He hears your heart and is actively working in your life and circumstances, even if His plans unfold in ways you may not expect.

Lessons within the Lesson:

List the thought-provoking verses or statements that spoke to you in this chapter.

Which statement may have the utmost impact on your prayer life?

How will your prayer life change because of this statement?

List the steps you will take to make the changes necessary to strengthen your prayer life.

17: UNDERSTANDING GOD'S WILL

1 John 5:14-15 (NIV), Romans 12:1-2 (NKJV)

Opening Prayer:

Our Heavenly Father, I come before You with a humble heart, seeking to understand and follow Your perfect will for my life. I recognize that Your plans are higher than mine, and Your wisdom surpasses my understanding. Lord, I surrender my desires to You. Help me to be open to Your leading and guidance, even when different from what I initially thought or hoped for. Grant me the clarity to discern Your path and the strength to follow it, even when it seems challenging. May Your will be my anchor, the foundation upon which I build my life. In times of uncertainty, help me to trust in Your sovereignty and love. Let Your peace guard my heart and mind In Jesus' name, I pray. Amen!

Today's Bible Verse: **1 John 5:14-15 (NIV), Romans 12:1-2 (NKJV)**

This is the confidence we have in approaching God: that if we ask anything according to his will, he hears us. And if we know that he hears us — whatever we ask — we know that we have what we asked of him (1 John 5:14-15, NIV).

I beseech you therefore, brethren, by the mercies of God, that you present your bodies a living sacrifice, holy, (and) acceptable to God, which is your reasonable service. And do not be conformed to this world, but be transformed by the renewing of your mind, that you may prove what is that good and acceptable and perfect will of God (ROMANS 12:1-2).

Associated Scriptures:

But if we walk in the light, as he is in the light, we have fellowship with one another, and the blood of Jesus, his Son, purifies us from all sin (1 John 1:7).

But I say, walk by the Spirit, and you will not carry out the desire of the flesh. For the flesh sets its desire against the Spirit, and the Spirit against the flesh; for these are in opposition to one another, so that you may not do the things that you please (Galatians 5:16-17).

But if anyone obeys his word, God's love is truly made complete in him. This is how we know we are in him: Whoever claims to live in him must walk as Jesus did (1 John 2:5-6).

Correlative Quotes:

God's compassion has been described in detail in the first 11 chapters of Romans. The content of Paul's urging is to offer your bodies (cf. Romans 6:13) as living sacrifices. A Christian's body is the temple of the Holy Spirit (1 Corinthians 6:19-20).[56] – Walvoord and Zuck

The world wants to control your mind, but God wants to transform your mind (Ephesians 4:17-24). This word transform is the same as transfigure in Matthew 17:2. It has come into our English language as the word "metamorphosis." It describes a change from within.[57]   Wiersbe

But after all, the true preservative of believers against 'conformity to the world,' is to 'be renewed in the spirit of their mind.' It is the lively presence and ruling power of the positive element that will alone effectually keep out of the heart the negative one.[58] – Jamieson, Fausset, Brown

---

[56] John Walvoord and Roy B. Zuck, The Bible Knowledge Commentary, N. T., Ibid.

[57] Warren Wiersbe, The Wiersbe Bible Commentary: N. T, Ibid., P. 441-442.

[58] Robert Jamieson, A.R. Fausset, David Brown, Commentary Critical and Explanatory on the Whole Bible, Public Domain, Ibid., P. 252.

Author's Notes:

INTRODUCTION

Romans 12:1-2 is a powerful and pivotal passage from the New Testament. It addresses the concept of transformation by regeneration in our minds in the context of living by God's will. Transformation commences with salvation (Romans 5:1). We become a new creation in Christ Jesus (2 Corinthians 5:17). Spiritual renewal represents the action of sanctification through spiritual growth (1 John 1:9).

TWO SIMPLE TRUTHS FROM THESE VERSES:

TRUTH #1:

That if we ask anything according to His will, God hears us. If we know that He hears us, whatever we ask, we know that we have what we asked of Him (1 John 5:14-15).

When we pray in the will of God, He gives us what we ask!

Here in this verse, we demonstrate our confidence in approaching God. In this simple statement, we see why and how we should pray. We can't approach God physically. We must come to Him through prayer. However, we must ask in Jesus' name. Secondly, He requires believers to be in and ask for His will.

TRUTH #2:

You desire but do not have, so you kill. You covet but you cannot get what you want, so you quarrel and fight. You do not have because you do not ask God. When you ask, you do not receive, because you ask with wrong motives, that you may spend what you get on your pleasures (James 4:2-3).

When we pray outside God's will, we don't get what we ask!

THE SOVEREIGN WILL OF GOD

Who has known the mind of the Lord so as to instruct him (1 Corinthians 2:16)?

The sovereignty of God asserts His absolute authority, control, and supremacy over all aspects of creation. His will and actions explain His complete and unchanging character. It encompasses every event, circumstance, and decision occurring in the universe. Understanding God's will is foundational in many religious and philosophical discussions. It is the foundational truth of Christianity. Here are key points explaining this concept:

DIVINE AUTHORITY: MATTHEW 28:28

Jesus said: *all authority is given to me.* The sovereign will of God asserts His supreme authority over all creation. This dominion means that God's decisions and plans are the ultimate authority, and nothing can happen contrary to His will. Nothing!.

DIVINE PLAN: PROVERBS 19:2

The concept of God's sovereignty will often include the idea that He has a comprehensive plan for creation. God states through Solomon: *Many plans are in a man's heart, but the counsel of the Lord will stand.* This plan encompasses the beginning, the end, and everything in between. Every action, no matter how insignificant, is part of this divine plan.

TRUST AND SUBMISSION: JAMES 4:7

Believers often view the concept of God's sovereignty as a reason for trust and submission. James 4:7 suggests: *Submit yourselves, then, to God. Resist the devil, and he will flee from you.* This verse means that even in challenging or confusing circumstances, there's a belief that God's overarching plan is ultimately for good.

DIVINE PROVIDENCE: ROMANS 8:28

The concept of divine providence is closely related to God's sovereign will. The apostle Paul says through the Spirit: *we know that all things work together for good to them that love God, who are the called according to His purpose* (NKJV). It suggests God is actively involved in the world, guiding events according to His desires and provision for His creation.

MYSTERY AND HUMAN UNDERSTANDING:

The full scope of God's sovereignty lies beyond human comprehension. Many acknowledge the mysteries regarding God's reign and how He interacts with human experiences and choices. Few, however,

ever experience the complete comfort they bring.

The authority of God varies among different religious traditions and theological perspectives. While the concept is a cornerstone of Judaism and Christianity, how it operates and interacts with human affairs can be the subject of profound theological discussions.

THE PRACTICAL WILL OF GOD

God not only has a sovereign will, but He also has a practical will. God commands us to live according to His representative of obedience, Jesus. This practical will is God's will of submission and obedience. When we ask in His will, we will receive.

URGE IN VIEW OF GOD'S MERCY:

The passage begins with a strong prompting concerning God's mercy. Paul urges believers to respond to God's mercy. They have received grace from God through Christ's death, burial, and resurrection. This mercy is the foundation for the transformative process that follows.

OFFER YOUR BODIES AS A LIVING SACRIFICE:

1 John 5:14-15 signifies a radical commitment. Believers have received a call to dedicate their lives entirely to God. This call resembles the sacrificial offering as consecrated in the Old Testament. However, this offering is not a physical sacrifice but a spiritual commitment of one's entire being. True and proper worship describes offering one's life as a life-giving sacrifice (Romans 12:1-2) and is touted as true and proper worship. This concept expands the traditional understanding of worship beyond rituals and ceremonies to a life surrendered to God's will.

NON-CONFORMITY TO THE WORLD:

Believers are instructed through Romans 12:1-2 not to conform to the patterns and values of the world. This verse highlights the need for a distinct, counter-cultural lifestyle rooted in God's values. True transformation begins with a renewal of the mind. Spiritual growth implies a fundamental change in thinking, beliefs, and perspective. It's a transformative process that aligns the mind with God's truth and righteousness.

DISCERNING GOD'S WILL:

As a result of this transformation, believers gain discernment and perform God's will for their lives. These actions are significant because They indicate changes leading to a deeper understanding of God's intentions and the ability to live in accordance with them.

GOD'S GOOD, PLEASING, AND PERFECT WILL:

Paul emphasizes that God's will is not arbitrary or restrictive; rather, it is good, pleasing, and perfect. This reassures believers that living in God's will brings fulfillment and aligns with what is truly beneficial. All good gifts come from God (James 1:17). However, 1 Thessalonians 5:18 teaches us to be thankful in all situations of life: *give thanks in all circumstances; for this is God's will for you in Christ Jesus.*

Spiritual Application:

> The fact of frail, feeble man so proudly ordering his own life and forgetting God, seems to the apostle James (James 4:13-17) so preposterous that he scarcely deems it worthwhile to argue the point, he only says, *Go to now*[59]! – Spurgeon

Romans 12:1-2 is a call to radical transformation and devotion to God. It emphasizes the importance of renewing the mind, non-conformity to the world, and the resulting ability to discern God's perfect will. This passage is a cornerstone for understanding the practical implications of faith in daily living and pursuing God's purposes for life change.

Lessons within the Lesson:

List the thought-provoking verses or statements that spoke to you in this chapter.

Which statement may have the utmost impact on your prayer life?

How will your prayer life change because of this statement?

List the steps you will take to make the changes necessary to strengthen your prayer life.

---

[59] Charles Spurgeon, God's Will About the Future, spurgeongems.com. Public Domain, P. 1.

18: GOD'S WILL AND HIS OMNIPOTENCE

Ephesians 1:19-23

Opening Prayer:

I come before You in awe of Your limitless strength and boundless might. You are the Creator of the universe, the One who spoke galaxies into existence and holds all things together by Your Word. Help me to remember that You are in control, even when circumstances seem overwhelming. Grant me the faith to believe that Your plans are perfect and that Your power is at work in every situation. When doubts arise, may I be reminded of Your might, and may my heart be filled with confidence in Your sovereign authority. Your power knows no bounds, and You reign over all creation. Thank You for refuge, strength, and unwavering power. Your power is my assurance, my anchor, and my hope. In Jesus' name, I pray. Amen!

Today's Bible Verse: Ephesians 1:19-23.

And his incomparably great power for us who believe. That power is like the working of his mighty strength, which he exerted in Christ when he raised him from the dead and seated him at his right hand in the heavenly realms, far above all rule and authority, power and dominion, and every title that can be given, not only in the present age but also in the one to come. And God placed all things under his feet and appointed him to be head over everything for the church, which is his body, the fullness of him who fills everything in every way (Ephesians 1:19-23).

> *Indeed before the day was, I am He; And there is no one who can deliver out of My hand; I work, and who will reverse it?* (Isaiah 43:13).

> *By his power God raised the Lord from the dead, and he will raise us also* (1 Corinthians 6:14).

> *For the Spirit God gave us does not make us timid, but gives us power, love and self-discipline* (1 Timothy 1:7).

Correlative Quotes:

It is enough to raise Christ from the dead, a tremendous power. Not only is it resurrection power, but it is the power that set Christ at God's right hand, and that is ascension power. The power that took Christ to the right hand of God is the same power that is available to believers today. That is why Paul prays that believers may know the greatness of that power. He writes: *that I may know him, the power of his resurrection* (Philippians 3:10).[60] – McGee

The transcendent, immeasurable, more than sufficient greatness of his dynamic power. Paul heaps up terms that defy description and Speaking of God's power. We can depend on God's power. It is divine, inexhaustible, irreversible, and available. No one need ever complain of insufficient power to meet temptations, to overcome sinful habits, or to live and witness for Christ.[61] – Roustio

There are many articles of faith contained in this passage, that Christ died, that he is raised from the dead, that he was raised from the dead by God the Father, and that his resurrection was by the power of God: the resurrection of any person is an instance of great power, but Christ's resurrection from the dead was an instance of peculiar and special power; for he was raised from the dead as a public person, representing all his people, for whom he became a surety; and he was raised

---

[60] J. Vernon McGee, Through the Bible with J. Vernon McGee, Vol. 5, Ibid., P.229.
[61] Edward R. Roustio, Liberty Bible Commentary, Ibid. P. 2408.

again for their justification, and to great glory in himself, after he had been brought into a very low estate.[62] – Gill

Author's Notes:

INTRODUCTION

Ephesians 1:19-23 (ESV) provides a rich passage to analyze and understand God's omniscience. The depth and breadth of His incredible knowledge, particularly within the broader context of His divine attributes, overwhelms the human mind. Let's explore how His great and unmatched wisdom relates to His all-knowing nature.

> *I am God, and there is no other; I am God, and there is none like me, declaring the end from the beginning and from ancient times things not yet done, saying, My counsel shall stand, and I will accomplish all my purpose* (Isaiah 46:9-10, ESV).

THE POWER OF GOD'S WILL: ISAIAH 43:13

God's sovereignty depends in part on His omnipotence, His all-powerful nature. He says: *Even from eternity I am He, and there is none who can deliver out of My hand; I act and who can reverse it?* This power means God can execute His will without limitation. His might extends to every aspect of existence. No one can thwart the will of God. He is all-powerful.

THE IMMEASURABLE GREATNESS OF HIS POWER

> *Great is our Lord, and abundant in power; his understanding is beyond measure* (Psalm 147:5, ESV).

The passage in Ephesians begins by emphasizing the immeasurable greatness of God's power. This power is evident in the resurrection of Christ, showcasing God's authority over life and death. This unmatched depth of His sovereignty typifies and enhances His omniscience.

God has the knowledge required to control and manipulate the fabric of life beyond human comprehension. Our God is powerful beyond belief and understanding. We cannot envision its scope. Proverbs 21:30

---

[62] John Gill, John Gill's Exposition of the Entire Bible, Ibid., P. 5004.

states: *There is no wisdom, no insight, no plan that can succeed against the LORD.*

ABSOLUTE POWER:

Omnipotence suggests that God possesses a power beyond human comprehension or limitation. This power includes the ability to do anything logically impossible, not limited by the laws of nature or the physical constraints that humans face.

LOGICAL LIMITATIONS:

The concept of omnipotence does not necessarily imply that God can do logically contradictory things. However, omnipotence does not extend to performing inherently self-contradictory actions.

GOD'S WILL DEALING WITH GOODNESS AND EVIL:

The existence of evil and suffering in the world has led to philosophical challenges regarding God's omnipotence. God's will could preclude suffering of any kind. However, His justice confines godly actions to those who believe in the payment made for them and their obedience to love Him and others.

Spiritual Application:

God remains all-powerful. It was His will to create all in existence. He completed creation (Genesis 1:31). However, God continues to maintain his plan and purpose. Humanity cannot destroy it or explain away His existence. God will be himself. Human intellect will not sway Him.

Lessons within the Lesson:

List the thought-provoking verses or statements that spoke to you in this chapter.

Which statement may have the utmost impact on your prayer life?

How will your prayer life change because of this statement?

List the steps you will take to make the changes necessary to strengthen your prayer life.

19: GOD'S WILL AND HIS OMNIPRESENCE

Jeremiah 23:24, NASB

Opening Prayer:

> Help me, Lord, to be patient in waiting for Your timing. I recognize that Your timing is perfect, and though I may not fully comprehend it, I trust that Your ways are higher than mine. May Your will be the anchor that steadies my soul in times of uncertainty. Grant me the strength to embrace Your will, even when it challenges my comfort or understanding. Mold my heart to echo the words of Jesus, saying, "Not my will, but Yours be done." As I pray for my needs and the needs of others, let Your will be the driving force behind my requests. Let Your glory shine through my prayers, and allow Your purposes fulfillment in every situation. I yield my heart to Your will, confident that Your plans are always for my good and Your glory. In Jesus' name, I pray. Amen!

Today's Bible Verse: Jeremiah 23:24, NASB

> *Can a man hide himself in hiding places so I do not see him? declares the Lord. Do I not fill the heavens and the earth? declares the Lord.*

Associated Scriptures:

> *The eyes of the Lord are in every place, watching the evil and the good* (Proverbs 15:3).

> *But will God indeed dwell on the earth? Behold, heaven and the highest heaven cannot contain You, how much less this house which I have built!* (1 Kings i:27, NASB).

Where can I go from Your Spirit? Or where can I flee from Your presence? If I ascend to heaven, You are there; If I make my bed in Sheol, behold, You are there. If I take the wings of the dawn, If I dwell in the remotest part of the sea (Psalm 139:7-9)

Correlative Quotes:

The false prophets misunderstood the character of God. He was not some localized God from whom a prophet could hide so God could not see him. Indeed, God in His omniscience fills heaven and earth so that no place is outside His realm. He had heard what the prophets said when they spoke lies in His name.[63] – Walvoord and Zuck

Jehovah wasn't a local deity like the pagan idols, but a transcendent God who reigns above all things and fills heaven and earth (vv. 23-24). Nor was He blind like the idols (Psalms 115:5), unable to see the sins of the people. "Can any hide himself in secret places that I shall not see him?" (Jeremiah 23:24) Because they listened to the false prophets, the people believed lies about God, and what we believe about God determines how we live.[64] – Wiersbe

A reason is given why the false prophets should not be heeded; they have not stood in the counsels of Yahweh-an image from ministers present, in a standing posture, at councils of Eastern kings. The spiritual man alone has the privilege, as Abraham had.[65] – Jamieson, Fausset, and Brown

Author's Notes:

INTRODUCTION

In Jeremiah 23:24, the prophet captures the profound truth of our Lord's omnipresence and all-encompassing nature (Psalm 95:4-5). It is God's nature to create. Colossians 1:16 states: *For in him all things were created: things in heaven and on earth, visible and invisible, whether*

---

[63] John Walvoord and Roy B. Zuck, The Bible Knowledge Commentary, O. T.

[64] Warren Wiersbe, The Wiersbe Bible Commentary: O. T., Ibid. P. 1237-8.

[65]Robert Jamieson, A.R. Fausset, David Brown, Commentary Critical and Explanatory on the Whole Bible, Public Domain, Vol. IV. Jeremiah—Malach, P. 66.

thrones or powers or rulers or authorities; all things have been created through him and for him.

IMPOSSIBILITY OF HIDING:

Jeremiah, writing under the inspiration of God's Spirit begins this dialogue with a rhetorical question: *Can a man hide himself in secret places so that I cannot see him?* The answer is implied: No, a person cannot hide from God's sight, no matter how secret or hidden their location may be. This emphasizes God's omniscience. His all-knowing nature finds us wherever we are. The old saying reads: *You can run, but you can't hide.* This statement applies uniquely to God. His awareness extends beyond mere physical sight to encompass a deep understanding of the thoughts, intentions, and actions of every individual.

FILLING HEAVEN AND EARTH:

The second part of the verse asserts, "Do I not fill heaven and earth?" This statement underscores the concept of God's omnipresence — that He exists everywhere in His creation. He is not limited by space or time. Instead, He encompasses all dimensions and every corner of the universe. He is immanent (present within creation) and transcendent (beyond and above all things).

DECLARATION OF THE LORD:

The verse concludes with the repeated proclamation, "declares the LORD." This ending emphasizes the divine authority and certainty of the statement. The Lord Himself is affirming His presence and knowledge.

IMPLICATIONS OF GOD'S OMNIPRESENCE:

Jeremiah 23:24 reveals the foundational truth of God's omnipresence and has several profound implications. For instance, God's omnipresence comforts believers, assuring them that they are never truly alone and that God is with them even in their innermost thoughts and struggles. It emphasizes God's sovereignty, as His presence extends everywhere, demonstrating His rule over everything.

This verse serves as a reminder of the futility of attempting to hide from God's sight. The Lord sees and knows where we are or what we do. The Maker of all things and Judge of all humanity is present everywhere.

Verse 24 also calls for humility and reverence, recognizing that we are always in the presence of a holy and just God.

Spiritual Application:

Old Testament authors marvel at this idea: no matter where we go, God is there. Whether we visit the heights of heaven (Job 22:12), the depths of Sheol (Psalms 139:7-10), or the farthest reaches of creation (Psalm 40:28), God is there. He fixates on His handiwork (Hebrews 11:3). The Father does not sleep. Psalm 121:3-4 state unequivocally He who loves us and provides for our protection: *He will not let your foot slip. He who watches over you will not slumber; He does not become distracted. Indeed, He who watches over Israel will neither slumber nor sleep.*

Jeremiah 23:24 underscores the comforting and awe-inspiring reality that God's presence is a constant companion, offering guidance, protection, and a deep sense of connection to all who seek Him.

The words of these verses also beautifully encapsulate the idea of God's omnipresence. It reminds us that God's presence is not limited to a particular location or time. Instead, He permeates all creation, seeing and knowing all things. This verse is a powerful reflection of God's attributes and invites us to draw closer to Him with a profound sense of awe and humility.

Lessons within the Lesson:

List the thought-provoking verses or statements that spoke to you in this chapter.

Which statement may have the utmost impact on your prayer life?

How will your prayer life change because of this statement?

List the steps you will take to make the changes necessary to strengthen your prayer life.

20: GOD'S WILL AND HIS OMNISCIENCE

Psalm 139:4 (NASB)

Opening Prayer:

Our God and Father, I come before You with a humble heart, seeking to understand and follow Your perfect will for my life. I recognize that Your plans are higher than mine. Your wisdom surpasses my understanding. Lord, I surrender my desires. I disregard my plans and look to You. Help me open my mind to Your leadership and guidance, even when it may differ from what I initially thought or hoped for. Grant me the clarity to discern Your path and the strength to follow it, even though Your directions may challenge me. In Christ's matchless name, I pray. Amen!

Today's Bible Verse: **Psalm 139:4 (NASB).**

Even before there is a word on my tongue, Behold, LORD, You know it all.

Associated Scriptures:

If our hearts condemn us, we know that God is greater than our hearts, and he knows everything (1 John 3:20).

Great is our Lord and mighty in power; his understanding has no limit (Psalm 147:5, NKJV).

O Lord, You have searched me and known me. You know when I sit down and when I rise up; You understand my thought from afar. You scrutinize my path and my lying down, and are intimately acquainted with all my ways. (Psalm 139:1-4).

Correlative Quotes:

The great controversy which for many ages has divided the Christian church has hinged upon the difficult question of "the will." I need not say of that conflict that it has done much mischief to the Christian church, undoubtedly it has, but I will rather say, that it has been fraught with incalculable usefulness, for it has thrust forward before the minds of Christians, precious truths, which, but for it, might have been kept in the shade.[66]   – Spurgeon

Author's Notes:

The Path of Life

As I walk along this road,
And think about the heavy load,
Of past and present sins I've done,
The guilt once walked is now a run.

Oh how can one deep in pain,
Ever find relief again.
How is it possible to find,
A savior who is good and kind.

One who understands my life,
Filled with worldly sin and strife.
I must admit I am ashamed,
I won the toss but lost the game.

Then I see in a world that harms,
One who'll hold me in His arms.
A Lord and Savior from the cross.
Who paid the price for all the lost.

His love transcends my sinful way,
He calls my name and it's ok.
He saves me from the depths of sin.
He opens the door, to let me in.

Psalm 139 as a whole reaches into the depths of the human experience. It acknowledges God's awareness of every facet of our lives. The psalmist explores Jehovah's presence in every moment. He knows all

---

[66] Charles Spurgeon, God's Will and Man's Will, Message #442, spurgeongems.org. Public Domain, P. 1.

of humanity from the depths of darkness to the heights of heaven.

In verse 4 (*Behold Lord, You know it all*), the focus narrows to the spoken word. Our words are an expression of the mind communicated for the benefit, positive or negative, of others. The scriptural insert in verse 4, *you know it all*, emphasizes that His knowledge remains comprehensive and all encompassing. The words we speak reflect the unspoken intentions behind them.

The rich meaning within the context of this remarkable Psalm explores the Omniscient One. The one who reigns understands everything beyond the surface, penetrating the innermost recesses of our hearts and minds. Through this lens, we will gain insight into the depth of His intimate knowledge of us and how it impacts our relationship with Him. The maker who owns everything always expresses His will in words and actions. Here we see His omniscience through a single verse. His will remains the same. His plans cannot be broken. His knowledge exceeds the wisest person.

THE SON'S RELATIONSHIP TO THE FAITH

> *Looking unto Jesus, the author and finisher of our faith, who for the joy that was set before Him endured the cross, despising the shame, and has sat down at the right hand of the throne of God* (Hebrews 12:2).

God has placed Jesus far above all rule and authority. This passage in Hebrews asserts Christ's superiority over all rule, authority, power, and dominion, both in the present and future ages. God's omniscience is apparent in His complete awareness of every hierarchical structure and governance, visible or hidden. The knowledge of God confuses unbelieving and unfaithful humanity.

SEATED AT GOD'S RIGHT HAND

> *The reason my Father loves me is that I lay down my life only to take it up again* (John 10:17)

The passage mentions Christ being raised from the dead and seated at God's right hand in heavenly places. This transformative action, the punishment, death, burial, and resurrection of His Son Jesus, symbolizes God's exalted position and authority over all realms. It highlights God's ultimate rule over all creation, especially life itself. His supremacy exemplifies the interconnection between the power in creation and omniscience. An all-knowing God governs with wisdom and understanding.

GOD'S OMNISCIENCE IMPACTS US DIRECTLY

Romans 8:11 explains this power of the resurrection by describing it in more detail. The apostle Paul explains: *And if the Spirit of him who raised Jesus from the dead is living in you, he who raised Christ from the dead will also give life to your mortal bodies through his Spirit, who lives in you.*

We represent the product of God's ingenuity. Because God knows all outcomes, He planned everything before the foundation of the world (Ephesians 1:3-60. Praise be to the God and Father of our Lord Jesus. God's will determined Christ's life, death, and resurrection. His purpose became our salvation. We are the grateful recipients of His grace.

Spiritual Application:

Nestled within the verses of Psalm 139, verse 4 stands as a powerful declaration of God's omniscience. The verse reads: *Even before a word is on my tongue, behold, O LORD, you know it altogether*. This compact statement captures the essence of the Psalm's overarching theme, God's all-knowing nature. It invites us to reflect on the profound reality that God's understanding transcends our spoken words. His omnipotence, omnipresence, and omniscience allow God to express His will in terms of the needs of each individual.

Lessons within the Lesson:

List the thought-provoking verses or statements that spoke to you in this chapter.

Which statement may have the utmost impact on your prayer life?

How will your prayer life change because of this statement?

List the steps you will take to make the changes necessary to strengthen your prayer life.

21. QUESTION #3: HOW ARE WE TO PRAY?

Psalm 72:12

Opening Prayer: (The prayer for today is adapted from Psalms 51:10-14).

> Create in me a pure heart, O God, and renew a faithful spirit within me. Do not cast me from Your presence. Restore in me daily the joy of Your grace, the comfort of Your salvation, and grant me a willingness to serve You alone. Sustain me with Your power. Then I will teach transgressors your ways, and sinners will turn to you. Alleviate the feelings of guilt haunting me from past sins. You, O Lord, have rescued me. You are the God who saves me. My tongue will sing of your righteousness forever. I open my mind to You. Search me and find me to be true. In Your Son's blessed name, I pray. Amen!

Today's Bible Verse: **Psalm 72:12.**

> *For He will deliver the needy who cry out, the afflicted who have no one to help.*

Associated Scriptures:

> *The LORD will fight for you; you need only to be still* (Exodus 14:14).

> *For those who are led by the Spirit of God are the children of God* (Romans 8:14).

> *If we confess our sins, he is faithful and just to forgive us our sins and to cleanse us from all unrighteousness. If we say we have no sin we make Him a liar and the truth is not in us* (1 John 1:9-10).

Correlative Quotes:

THIS is a royal psalm. In it you see predictions of Christ, not upon the cross, but upon the throne. In reference to His manhood as well as to His Godhead, He is exalted and extolled, and very high. He is the King—the King's Son, truly, with absolute sway, stretching His scepter from sea to sea, and "from the river even unto the ends of the earth." It is remarkable that in this psalm which so fully celebrates the extent of His realm, and the sovereignty of His government, there is so much attention drawn to the minuteness of His care for the lowly, His personal sympathy with the poor, and the large benefits they are to enjoy from His kingdom.[67]   – Spurgeon

One blessing, however, that will always come to God's needy ones is this—Christ will right them, He will judge them with judgement.[68] – Spurgeon

Oh, what glorious comfort there is in this! We shall be spared, we shall be redeemed, we shall be delivered, we shall be saved, we shall be revenged and cleared before the judgment-bar of God, and all because the great King has made the poor and needy the special objects of His love.[69] – Spurgeon

Author's Notes:

INTRODUCTION

If there is any place where the "do so more and more" applies, it is in our devotion to prayer.[70] – Piper

The Bible guides us in how to pray to God, emphasizing sincerity, humility, and a heart-focused connection. While there isn't a specific

---

[67] Charles Spurgeon, The Poor Man's Friend, Sermon # 1037, Public Domain, spurgeonsgems.org. P. 1.

[68] Charles Spurgeon, Ibid., P. 5.

[69] Charles Spurgeon, Ibid., P. 6.

[70] John Piper, How to Pray, By John Piper. © Desiring God Foundation. Source: desiringGod.org., Fair Use Authorization, Section 107, of the Copyright Law, desiringgod.org/messages/god-so-loved-the-world-part-1.

formula for prayer, the Bible contains many principles and examples of how to pray. God's Word will help guide believers in their prayer lives. Not knowing how to pray or learning to pray should not stop us from praying. Since prayer is talking with God, we should know where to start. Praise Him. God gave your life.

PRAY FOR SINCERITY AND WITH AUTHENTICITY:

> God, grant me the serenity to accept the things I cannot change, courage to change the things I can, and wisdom to know the difference.[71] – Reinhold Niebuhr

Prayer should come from the heart. We should express genuine thoughts, feelings, and desires. Jesus emphasized the importance of sincerity in Matthew 6:5-6, encouraging private and heartfelt prayer rather than seeking public attention.

Authentic prayers explain to God and others the true you. We could say: *We see the good, the bad, and the ugly.*

> God, you know our thoughts before we even think them. You know all the hurt, the aches we can't identify and the longings for what's real. You go there, Lord, and you beckon us to come with you into the beautiful deep. God, help us to go there with you. Amen.[72] – McDonald

APPROACH THE THRONE WITH HUMILITY:

We must recognize God's greatness and our dependence on HIm. Humility represents a key aspect of prayer. Jesus shared a parable about a tax collector (Luke 18:9-14). The Pharisee was proud and God rejected his prayer as a result of his pride. But the tax collector humbly approached God in prayer and was justified. If we ask, God will help us to not only to be humble but to pray with humility.

> *He guides the humble in what is right and teaches them*
> *his way* (Psalm 25:9).

---

[71] Meisha Johnson, Best Bible Verses for Serenity, psalm91.com/2020/08/26/best-verses-for-serenity/,, Used by permission, Fair Use Authorization, Section 107, of the Copyright Law P. 1.
[72] Abby McDonald, and excerpt from a prayer on authenticity, abbymcdonald.org/2015/10/a-prayer-for-authenticity/., Used by permission, Fair Use Authorization, Section 107, of the Copyright Law. P.1.

After his sin with Bathsheba, King David prays a heartfelt prayer of repentance in Psalm 51:

> Have mercy on me, O God, according to your unfailing love; according to your great compassion blot out my transgressions. Wash away all my iniquity and cleanse me from my sin (Psalm 51:1-2).

Through this prayer, David humbly acknowledges his wrongdoing, seeks God's forgiveness, and asks for a clean heart and renewed spirit.

CALL OUT TO GOD WITH ADORATION AND PRAISE:

Begin prayer by acknowledging God's attributes, sovereignty, and goodness. Expressing adoration and gratitude helps to set the tone for a meaningful connection with God (Psalm 100:4).

Psalm 100:4 demonstrates our responsibility to continually pray, especially when we enter the house of God. Since God is everywhere at once, He is present when we assemble for worship. God inhabits our prayers and our praises (Psalm 22:3).

> Enter his gates with thanksgiving and his courts with praise; give thanks to him and praise his name.

We are to *pray without ceasing* (1 Thessalonians).

CONFESS YOUR DISOBEDIENCE BEFORE HIM:

Confess your disobedience to God honestly. Confession fosters a sense of humility and a desire for forgiveness and transformation.

1 John 1:9 tells us, *If we confess our sins, he is faithful and just and will forgive us our sins and purify us from all unrighteousness..*

USE PETITION AND INTERCESSION:

Present your requests and needs before God. Intercede on behalf of others as well. While asking for personal needs is appropriate, balanced prayer also includes concerns for others.

1 Timothy 2:1 explains our responsibly when Paul explains to Timothy: *I urge, then, first of all, that petitions, prayers, intercession and thanksgiving be made for all people.* These instructions to the young pastor were vital for his growth as a leader. These prayers maintain unity.

PRAY IN GOD'S WILL AND SUBMISSION:

Seek alignment with God's will. Jesus prayed, Not my will, but yours be done (Luke 22:42). It's essential to be open to God's will and plan even when it differs from your desires.

> *Father, if you are willing, take this cup from me; yet not my will, but yours be done.*

PRACTICE PERSISTENT PETITIONING:

Jesus encouraged persistence in prayer (Luke 11:5-13). While not about repetitive words, this teaches the importance of persevering in bringing your needs and concerns before God.

> *I tell you, even though he will not get up and give you the bread because of friendship, yet because of your shameless audacity he will surely get up and give you as much as you need.*

> *So I say to you: Ask and it will be given to you; seek and you will find; knock and the door will be opened to you. For everyone who asks receives; the one who seeks finds; and to the one who knocks, the door will be opened (Luke 11:8-10).*

SHOW GRATITUDE:

Continually express thankfulness for answered prayers and blessings. Gratitude maintains a positive perspective and acknowledges God's provision (Colossians 4:2).

> *Devote yourselves to prayer, being watchful and thankful.*

LISTENING AND WAITING:

Prayer is not just speaking; it's also about listening to God. Spend quiet moments in God's presence, allowing time for His guidance and insights to come through (Psalm 46:10).

> *Be still, and know that I am God. I will be exalted among the nations, I will be exalted in the earth.*

USE SCRIPTURE WHEN PRAYING:

Incorporate biblical passages and teachings into your prayers. God's Word provides guidance and inspiration, allowing His communication with Him (Psalm 119:105).

> *Your Word is a lamp for my feet,*
> *A light on my path.*

Almighty God, You say in Psalms, Your Word provides light on my path. Please show me the light. Help me to follow in Your path of righteousness. Protect me from the evil hiding silently in the darkness. In Jesus' name, I ask. Amen.

Spiritual Application:

Remember that prayer is a personal and dynamic conversation with God. These principles provide a foundation, but there's room for individuality and variation in how you express your thoughts, emotions, and needs to Him. It's a relationship-building process based on your level of faith and understanding. Develop a consistent prayer routine (Matthew 6:6).

Lessons within the Lesson:

List the thought-provoking verses or statements that spoke to you in this chapter.

Which statement may have the utmost impact on your prayer life?

How will your prayer life change because of this statement?

List the steps you will take to make the changes necessary to strengthen your prayer life.

22: PRAY IN THE SPIRIT

Romans 8:26

Opening Prayer:

I ask for the grace to accept Your accountability with gratitude, knowing You work all things together for good. Help me to remember Your plans are for my welfare and not for harm, to give me a future and hope. Thank You, Lord, for your unfailing love and the privilege of being a part of Your divine plan. Encourage me to live each day in alignment with Your will, seeking to bring glory to Your name. I will pray in and with Your Spirit, Lord. I will pray with persistence In Jesus presence I pray. Amen!

Today's Bible Verse: **Romans 8:26**

Likewise the Spirit also helps in our weaknesses. For we do not know what we should pray for as we ought, but the Spirit Himself makes intercession for us with groanings which cannot be uttered.

Associated Scriptures:

Therefore, there is now no condemnation for those who are in Christ Jesus (Romans 8:1).

Those who live according to the sinful nature have their minds set on what that nature desires; but those who live in accordance with the Spirit have their minds set on what the Spirit desires (Romans 8:5).

You, however, are controlled not by the sinful nature but by the Spirit, if the Spirit of God lives in you. And if anyone does not have the Spirit of Christ, he does not belong to Christ (Romans 8:9).

Correlative Quotes:

Not that the HOLY GHOST groans, but he gives a fervency of prayer in the souls of his people, which can only express itself in groans, not in words. Not that the HOLY GHOST makes intercession for them, (for this is the sole office of JESUS the High Priest,) but with them.[73] – Hawker

Not as the Son intercedes for them, apart from themselves, at the mercy-seat; but within themselves, by inspiring them with these unutterable (or, unuttered) groanings; and they are conscious that such deep and intense yearnings are from the Divine Spirit moving them and teaching them to pray. They may not still be able to put their requests of God into definite form, but they know that God knows the meaning of what his own Spirit has inspired.[74] – Spence and Exell

But not in vain are these groanings. For "the Spirit Himself" is in them, giving to the emotions which Himself has kindled the only language of which they are capable; so that though on our part they are the fruit of impotence to utter what we feel, they are at the same time the intercession of the Spirit Himself in our behalf.[75] – Jamieson, Fausset, Brown

Author's Notes:

INTRODUCTION

Now faith is confidence in what we hope for and assurance about what we do not seen (Hebrews 11:1).

In Romans 8, the role of the Holy Spirit is to help believers and brining hope and assurance in Christ. When we accept Jesus as Lord, the Spirit lives in us. He now becomes available to direct our lives.

---

[73] Robert Hawker, The Poor Man's New Testament Commentary, Volume 2, 1805, Public Domain, Printed by W. Nicholson, Warner Street, London. P. 115.

[74] H. D. M. Spence and Joseph S. Exell, The Pulpit Commentary, Public Domain, Funk & Wagnalls Company New York And Toronto, P. 112.

[75] Robert Jamieson, A.R. Fausset, David Brown, Commentary Critical and Explanatory on the Whole Bible, Ibid. P. 242.

THE HOLY SPIRIT'S ASSISTANCE:

> *Nevertheless, I tell you the truth. It is to your advantage*
> *that I go away; for if I do not go away, the Helper will not*
> *come to you; but if I depart, I will send Him to you* (John
> 16:7, NKJV).

The verse begins by highlighting the assistance of the Holy Spirit in the lives of believers (Romans 8:16). The Holy Spirit is depicted as a helper who comes to aid and support believers in their times of weakness. This speaks to the idea that believers are not left on their own, but have divine help and guidance.

HUMAN WEAKNESS:

> *But you shall receive power when the Holy Spirit has*
> *come upon you; and you shall be witnesses to Me in*
> *Jerusalem, and in all Judea and Samaria, and to the end*
> *of the earth* (Acts 1:8, NKJV).

This verse in Romans 8 acknowledges human limitations and weaknesses. It states that there are times when believers might not know how to pray effectively or even know what to pray for. This lack of knowledge is a recognition of the challenges and uncertainties that believers face in their spiritual journeys.

INTERCESSION OF THE SPIRIT:

> *You gave Your good Spirit to instruct them, Your manna*
> *You did not withhold from their mouth, And You gave*
> *them water for their thirst* (Nehemiah 9:20).

Despite our limitations in understanding and proper use for prayer. Verse 26 of Romans 8 emphasizes the Holy Spirit's work of mediation on behalf of believers. We cannot overestimate the value He provides. Intercession, as described in chapter 8, refers to the Holy Spirit advocating, pleading, or intervening on behalf of believers before God. Arbitration, as described in the chapter, relies on *groanings that cannot be uttered.* This spiritual communication between the Spirit and the additional members of the triune Godhead indicates a deep, profound spiritual connection beyond words.

SPIRITUAL COMMUNICATION:

> *Do not be afraid, Daniel. Since the first day that you set your mind to gain understanding and to humble yourself before your God, your words were heard, and I have come in response to them* (Daniel 10:12).

Since God knows all things, He has heard our prayers even before we pray them.

In Romans 8:26 the Holy Spirit's provides a path to God. He establishes a form of communication beyond our ability to understand. The language of God. This conduit of carrying our desires suggests a direct, spiritual connection between the believer and God through the Holy Spirit's interceding work. The Spirit produces a direction connection. It is instantaneous. Before we think the need, the Spirit knows understands the situation, and God has already answered.

Spiritual Application:

Romans 8:26 encourages believers. This verse assures them in times of weakness or uncertainty. The Holy Spirit is actively involved in their spiritual lives. The Holy Spirit bridges the gap between human limitations and the Divine, helping believers in their prayers and serving as a conduit for communication between them and God. This verse speaks to the depth of the believer's relationship with God and the importance of relying on the guidance and support of the Holy Spirit.

Lessons within the Lesson:

List the thought-provoking verses or statements that spoke to you in this chapter.

Which statement may have the utmost impact on your prayer life?

How will your prayer life change because of this statement?

List the steps you will take to make the changes necessary to strengthen your prayer life.

23: PRAY WITHOUT HYPOCRISY

Matthew 6:5

<u>Opening Prayer</u>: (Today's prayer is adapted from Jeremiah 17:14-17.)

Heal me, O Lord, and I will be healed. Save me and I will be saved. You are the one I praise. My enemies keep ridiculing me by saying: *Where is the word of the Lord? Let it now be fulfilled*! But I have not allowed these words to dissuade me or cloud my thinking. I am your servant. Whatever I say, You hear. Treat me with love and concern. In Your Son's compassionate name, we pray. Amen!

<u>Today's Bible Verse</u>: **Matthew 6:5**

And when you pray, do not be like the hypocrites, for they love to pray standing in the synagogues and on the street corners to be seen by men. I tell you the truth, they have received their reward in full.

<u>Associated Scriptures</u>:

If my people who are called by my name humble themselves and pray and seek my face and turn from their wicked ways, then I will hear from heaven and will forgive their sin and heal their land (2 Chronicles 7:14, ESV).

For whoever exalts himself will be humbled, and he who humbles himself will be exalted (Luke 14:11, NKJV).

Let nothing be done through selfish ambition or conceit, but in lowliness of mind let each esteem others better than himself (Philippians 2:3, NKJV).

Correlative Quotes:

> It is not often that a man may safely speak about his own humility. Humble men are mostly conscious of great pride, while those who are boastful of humility have nothing but false pretense, and really lack and want it. I question whether any of us are at all judges as to our pride or humility. For pride so often assumes the shape of lowliness when it has its own end to serve.[76] – Spurgeon

> This verse expresses the negative result of this unity of soul that nothing will be done in *strife, nothing is done out of* factiousness nothing, that is, with the desire either of personal influence or of personal glory. For, he adds, *each will esteem other better than himself*, or, rather, will hold that his neighbor is worthy of higher consideration and a higher place of dignity than himself.[77] – Ellicott

> They prayed in the synagogues, which were indeed proper places for public prayer, but not for personal prayer. They pretended hereby to do honor to the place of their assemblies, but intended to *bring* honor to themselves. They prayed in the corners of the streets, the broad streets, (so the word signifies,) which were most frequented. They withdrew as if they were under a pious impulse which would not admit delay, but really it was to make themselves to be taken notice of.[78] – Henry

Author's Notes:

INTRODUCTION

Avoiding Hypocrisy became a central theme in Christ's teaching. In The Sermon on the Mount (Matthew 5 through 7), Jesus discusses using religious acts to gain social approval or status. True spirituality involves integrity, where inner beliefs align with outward actions. Some will receive

---

[76] Charles Spurgeon, Humility, Message #365, Public Domain, spurgeongems.org., P. 1.

[77] C. J. Ellicott, (Charles John), A New Testament Commentary for English Readers, 1819-1905. Public Domain,

[78] Matthew Henry, An Exposition of the Old and New Testament (Unabridged), Volume Vol V, (Matthew to John), Public Domain, Philadelphia : Ed. Harrington & Geo. D. Haswell, Market Street,1706, P. 63-64.

their earthly reward here and now (Matthew 6:2), others an eternal recompense in Heaven (Luke 6:23).

HISTORICAL BACKGROUND:

In Jesus' time, public displays of piety, such as elaborate public prayers, had become common. The Pharisees and other religious leaders commonly used public prayers for appearance and reputation. These verses in Matthew 6:5-8, within the context of the Savior's sermon critique, warn not to participate in this behavior.

LANGUAGE

The language used is direct and clear, cautioning against using the behavior of praying merely to be seen by others. Hypocrite refers to those who pretend to be devout but lack genuine faith.

CONTEXT

The Sermon on the Mount represents part of a larger section where Jesus is teaching his disciples about various aspects of righteous living (Matthew 5), giving to the needy (Matthew 6:1-4), including prayer (Matthew 6:5-15), fasting (Matthew 6:16-18), and building spiritual treasures, not earthly, (Matthew 6:1-4). The overall theme is sincerity and genuine devotion, as opposed to outward displays of religiosity.

PRAY WITHOUT HYPOCRISY:

When you pray in public, use the proper motive. The hypocrites pray to receive the recognition of those surrounding them. To them, the words are not as significant as the rationale. Religious people throughout history have demonstrated charitable acts and prayed loud and boisterous prayers in public. They hoped others would see them as pious. These Pharisaic pretenders chose to glorify themselves instead of bringing glory to the Father.

They corrupted and degraded the purpose of prayer. Many of these charlatans have confused the hearers. They rob others of the blessing of public prayer and submission to God and His glory. In Matthew 5:14-16, Jesus presents a picture of the believer spreading the light to all people. He says in verse 14: *In the same way, let your light shine before others, that they may see your good deeds and glorify your Father in heaven.*

A REWARD FOR RIGHTEOUSNESS

God will reward those with pure hearts (Matthew 6:4) desiring to praise and worship Him through public prayer. He will chasten those who seek to glorify themselves. Because those filled with pride are openly seeking self-aggrandizement, they have already received their reward (Matthew 6:2). He will bless those whose motive is to glorify him. A reward awaits those who love and serve others to the glory of God.

SINCERITY OF HEART

Christ's sermon emphasizes the importance of praying with sincerity and authenticity. Prayer should focus on the relationship between the individual and God rather than seeking recognition from others. While public worship has its place, Matthew 6:6 encourages private communion with God. Personal prayer allows for genuine expression and vulnerability before God without the distractions of public image.

Spiritual Application:

Matthew 6:5 underscores the importance of sincere, inward-focused prayer that stems from genuine faith and devotion. It serves as a reminder to approach spiritual practices with humility, integrity, and a desire for an authentic connection with God, rather than seeking praise from fellow humans.

Lessons within the Lesson:

List the thought-provoking verses or statements that spoke to you in this chapter.

Which statement may have the utmost impact on your prayer life?

How will your prayer life change because of this statement?

List the steps you will take to make the changes necessary to strengthen your prayer life.

24: PRAY PRIVATELY

Matthew 6:6

Opening Prayer:

God, our Father, You have promised to join me in my secret place of prayer. I believe and trust in the many promises You have made in the Scriptures. I know You are with me always. You live in me as Your Spirit has joined with mine, and we have become one in You. I realize Your concern for my well-being. Help me now in this time of need. All praise and honor belong to You. We praise Your name above all names. In Christ's name, I pray. Amen!

Today's Bible Verse: Matthew 6:6

But when you pray, go into your room, close the door and pray to your Father, who is unseen. Then your Father, who sees what is done in secret, will reward you.

Associated Scriptures:

Now when Daniel learned that the decree had been published, he went home to his upstairs room where the windows opened toward Jerusalem. Three times a day he got down on his knees and prayed, giving thanks to his God, just as he had done before (Daniel 6:10).

Be careful not to practice your righteousness in front of others to be seen by them. If you do, you will have no reward from your Father in heaven (Matthew 6:1).

Jesus prays alone, secluded: *Very early in the morning, while it was still dark, Jesus got up, left the house and went off to a solitary place, where he prayed* (Mark 1:35).

Correlative Quotes:

Jesus then spoke about the practice of prayer, which the Pharisees loved to perform publicly. Rather than making prayer a matter between an individual and God, the Pharisees had turned it into an act to be seen by men - again, to demonstrate their supposed righteousness. Their prayers were directed not to God but to other men, and consisted of long, repetitive phrases. Jesus condemned such practices. Prayer should be addressed to your Father, who is unseen (cf. John 1:18; 1 Timothy 1:17) and who knows what you need (Matthew 6:8); it is not "to be seen by men.[79] – Walvoord and Zuck

The word translated closet means "a private chamber." It could refer to the store chamber in a house. Our Lord prayed privately (Mark 1:35); so did Elisha (2 Kings 4:32ff) and Daniel (Daniel 6:10ff).[80] – Wiersbe

Of course, it is not the simple publicity of prayer which is here condemned. It may be offered in any circumstances, however open, if not prompted by the spirit of ostentation, but dictated by the great ending of prayer itself. It is the retiring character of true prayer which is here taught.[81] – Jamieson, Fausset, and Brown

Author's Notes:

INTRODUCTION

Jesus encouraged believers to pray privately in seclusion. When we have the opportunity, we should pray alone (Matthew 6:6). When you desire to pray for personal needs, it is best to be alone without worldly distractions.

---

[79] John Walvoord and Roy B. Zuck, The Bible Knowledge Commentary, N. T., Ibid., P. 32.

[80] Warren Wiersbe, The Wiersbe Bible Commentary: N. T., Ibid., P. 22.

[81] Robert Jamieson, A.R. Fausset, David Brown, Commentary Critical and Explanatory on the Whole Bible, Vol. II (Matthew-Romans), Public Domain, Ibid., P.25.

My ministry work for the Inland Empire Association in Riverside and San Bernardino counties (Southern California) as a church growth specialist requires me to spend considerable time in the car alone. I use this time to talk with God. I have experienced amazing results. For example, I have prayed for and seen miraculous interventions by the Spirit. Many times, I have encountered conflicts resolved before reaching a meeting. Correspondingly, small prayers like getting a green light at just the right time seem remarkable.

There is nothing too big or too small for God to rectify.

May car has become my secret place. At 80 years old (at the writing of this book), God's continual presence is reassuring. This union not only helps me, but it benefits others driving on the same highway.

We see in Matthew 6:6 a continuation of the teachings of Jesus in the Sermon on the Mount. This verse is also part of the theme of prayer and righteous living found in the Bible.

From the perspective of private prayer, this verse carries several significant points:

THE SETTING

The verse begins by suggesting a specific setting for prayer: *your room*. God encourages us in Matthew 6:6 to locate a quiet and secluded place where His disciples can focus solely on communication with God through prayer. Focus and uninterrupted time release His children from exasperating distractions separating us from the reality of life.

PRIVACY AND INTIMACY

The act of closing the door emphasizes the idea of privacy. This retreat to one's special quiet place is not about performing a show for others to view, but praying alone encourages establishing an intimate and personal connection with God. Luke 6:12 teaches: *One of those days Jesus went out to a mountainside to pray and spent the night praying to God..*

DIRECT COMMUNICATION WITH GOD

Matthew 6:6 expresses the directness of prayer. The quiet, isolated nature of solitary prayer builds a stronger relationship between the Maker and the disciple. We pray to God directly. It encourages individuals to pray to *their Father, who is unseen.* This insular prayer addresses the concept of God as a loving and caring presence who seeks connection unashamedly. Jesus suggests: *Come to me, all you who are weary and burdened, and I will give you rest. Take my yoke upon you and learn from me, for I am gentle and humble in heart, and you will find rest for your souls. For my yoke is easy and my burden is light* (Matthew 11:28-30).

The emphasis on privacy and the unseen nature of the interaction implies that this is a time for genuine communication. In private, there is no need to put on a facade or adhere to societal expectations. It's a space for raw, authentic expression.

RELATIONSHIP WITH GOD

Referencing God as "your Father" signifies a close and personal relationship. This approach to prayer reinforces the idea that prayer is not just a ritual but a conversation with a loving and understanding Creator.

THE PROMISE OF REWARD

The verse mentions the concept of reward for private prayer. This verse in Matthew does not refer to a material reward but rather the sense of fulfillment, spiritual growth, and a deepened connection with God that comes from sincere and private communication.

HUMILITY AND HUMBLENESS

Private prayer encourages humility by allowing individuals to approach God without asking for public recognition or validation. It's an opportunity to humble oneself before the Divine.

INNER TRANSFORMATION

Private prayer allows for self-reflection and introspection. It can lead to personal transformation as individuals confront their inner thoughts, *emotions, and struggles in the presence of God.*

SPIRITUAL DISCIPLINE

Regular private prayer becomes a spiritual discipline that nurtures the inner life and strengthens the individual's relationship with God over time.

FOCUS ON THE ETERNAL

By directing attention inward and heavenward, private prayer helps believers shift their focus from the transient and external to the eternal and internal. Our joy, for example, is different than our happiness. Happiness is external and temporal. Joy, however, is internal and eternal.

GOD'S IS SECRETE PLACE

Matthew 6:6b confirms the of the secret place concept when it says: *Then your Father, who sees what is done in secret, will reward you.*

When it says that the Father is in the secret place, it is referring to the idea that God is present and accessible in any physical location we happen to choose to pray and also in the hidden spaces of our hearts and inner lives. To understand the importance of this verse, we must study it in its context.

The Father *sees what is done in secret.* This statement means that He is intimately aware of and present in the depths of our hearts and minds. Since He is omnipresent, God also inhabits the secret place.

Our connection to God is in the inner recesses of our being where our thoughts, emotions, and intentions reside.

> *Hear my voice when I call, Lord; be merciful to me and answer me. My heart says of you, "Seek His face! Your face, Lord, I will seek. Do not hide your face from me, do not turn your servant away in anger; you have been my helper. Do not reject me or forsake me, God my Savior* (Psalm 27:7-9).

In this context, secret does not mean hidden from God. Instead, the hidden space is personal, intimate, and unfiltered. In our sheltered place, secluded from worldly issues and pressures, we cry out to Our Father through our spiritual connection. The emotions become real since we don't try to impress outsiders. These prayers exist between sinners who, saved by grace, petition their Lord. He rescued each believer from eternal punishment. In this place, they find solace in prayer.

GOD'S AWARENESS

Even though separated from the public eye, God knows all our thoughts, intentions, and prayers. He sees beyond outward actions and recognizes the true nature of His children's hearts.

PRIVATE CONNECTION

The verse emphasizes the value of personal and private communication with God. It encourages believers to engage in authentic, unguarded conversations with God in the quiet of their hearts.

REWARD IN THE SECRET:

The verse suggests that the rewards of sincere prayer probably remain unseen by the world but are experienced internally and spiritually. These rewards introduce followers to a deepened connection with God, inner peace, guidance, and personal transformation.

Spiritual Application:

Matthew 6:6 emphasizes the value of secluded prayer. Isolation fosters an authentic, intimate, and transformative relationship with God. This action-driven scripture encourages individuals to create a secure, private space for direct and sincere communication, free from external influences or appearances. This practice contributes to personal growth, a deepened connection with the Spirit, and a humble attitude toward the Trinity.

This transformative information shared by Jesus here in Matthew speaks of the Father being in the secret place. It emphasizes God's intimate connection with the hidden or forgotten depths of our being. It encourages believers to engage in private, sincere, and profound communication with God, recognizing that such a connection can lead to meaningful rewards beyond outward appearances. The term *secret place* reflects the intimacy of the relationship between an individual and God.

Lessons within the Lesson:

List the thought-provoking verses or statements that spoke to you in this chapter.

Which statement may have the utmost impact on your prayer life?

How will your prayer life change because of this statement?

List the steps you will take to make the changes necessary to strengthen your prayer life.

25: PRAY SUCCINCTLY

Matthew 6:7

Opening Prayer:

O Lord, I come into Your presence with humility. I recognize Your wisdom and understanding. It transcends all. I open my heart to Your love and my mind to Your will. Help me to pray without the weight of unnecessary words. You know my needs, even before I express them. You are aware of my desires, my hopes, and my fears. You continually assure me of Your love. I know You will listen, care, and respond to whatever I request within Your will. Grant me the grace to come to you just as I am, without pretense or masks. Your presence is my sanctuary, the place where my soul finds refuge. Know, Lord, I come directly to You, not with an abundance of words, but with the sincerity of a child approaching a loving parent. Grant me composure and tranquility in life and sanctity in death. In Jesus' name, I pray. Amen!

Today's Bible Verse: Matthew 6:7

And when you pray, do not keep on babbling like pagans, for they think they will be heard because of their many words.

Associated Scriptures:

Show me your ways, Lord, teach me your paths. Guide me in your truth and teach me, for you are God my Savior, and my hope is in you all day long (Psalm 25:4).

Lead me in Your truth and teach me, For You are the God of my salvation; For You, I wait all the day (Psalm 25:5, NASB).

Create in me a clean heart, O God, and renew a right spirit within me (Psalm 51:10).

Correlative Quotes:

Do not be imitators of *those who pray arduous long prayers*, and follow their ways, who have only the dim light of nature to guide them; it would be shameful in you to do as they do, when you have a divine revelation for your direction; and especially, because your Father knows what things ye have need of before ye ask him; and therefore have no need to make use of many words, or much speaking, or long prayers.[82] – Gill

Often He waits until we specifically ask Him. Sometimes He wants us to come to the end of our own pitiful resources before He intervenes. When we cry out in despair, He is honored as we express our complete dependence upon Him. Every prayer is the cry of a child saying, "Help, Father, I can't do this by myself."[83] – Prichard

God's response to our prayers is not governed by our wordy explanations of desire. It is governed by his knowledge of our real needs.[84] – Piper

Author's Notes:

INTRODUCTION

In Matthew 6:7 Jesus continues the teaching in the message entitled the Sermon on the Mount. This passage is part of His instruction on prayer and offers valuable insights into the nature of petitions and ordinary communication with God during informal asks. It stresses the importance of being succinct and not repetitive when we pray. He emphasizes the trinity's

---

[82] John Gill, John Gill's Exposition of the Entire Bible, 1810, Public Domain, Mathews & Leigh, London, P. 151.

[83] Ray Prichard, My God is Sovereign, Why Pray? preceptaustin.org/matthew_67-8#6:8. P. 1.

[84] John Piper, When God Answers No to Our Prayers, By John Piper. © Desiring God Foundation. Source: desiringGod.org , Used by permission, Fair Use Authorization, Section 107, of the Copyright Law,

omniscience as a reason for brevity and precision in talking with God. Since God knows our wants before our desires take shape, we don't need to be long-winded in our explanations.

PRAY SUCCINCTLY:

God doesn't need a long explanation detailing the situation surrounding your request. He is omniscient. Matthew 6:7: *And when you pray, do not keep on babbling like pagans, for they think they will be heard because of their many words.* God doesn't need a long explanation describing in detail the situation surrounding your request. He is omniscient.

Prayer is to be personal. When we talk with God, if we use repetitive prepared statements of our need or His praise, we are talking at Him. Conversational prayer should be brief and spontaneous. Jesus demonstrates the concept of planned prayer when He teaches the Apostles the Lord's Prayer. He says: *This, then, is how you should pray* (Matthew 6:9). This prayer represents an example of formal prayer. Jesus doesn't say this is what you should pray. He states instead how a believer should pray.

BE PERSISTENT IN PRAYER

Jesus explains the reason for and gives us an example of a short but dynamic prayer in the Lord's Prayer. He also suggests persistence in prayer. In Luke 11:5-8, the apostle quotes the Messiah when He says:

> *Then Jesus said to them: Suppose you have a friend, and you go to him at midnight and say, Friend, lend me three loaves of bread; a friend of mine on a journey has come to me, and I have no food to offer him.*

> *And suppose the one inside answers, 'Don't bother me. The door is already locked, and my children and I are in bed. I can't get up and give you anything.'*

> *I tell you, even though he will not get up and give you the bread because of friendship, yet because of your* **shameless audacity** *he will surely get up and give you as much as you need.*

Jesus says, in this example (and I paraphrase), Go to your friend next door at midnight. Say you have a visitor who has traveled a great distance and hasn't eaten. He asks: Can I have some food for him? The neighbor says: Go away, we are all in bed. I will have to climb over everyone to get what you want. He will not do it for you just because he is your friend, but because you persist, he will get up and get what you want.

Jesus uses the words shameless audacity when describing how the man in need should approach his neighbor. Jesus teaches us: Don't give up by thinking that God does not want to bless us. Your persistence shows God how deeply you feel the need for what you ask.

The neighbor wants to help. He will overcome the obstacles in his house once he realizes the seriousness of the situation. In clear inference to this example, God desires to help. He will answer the prayer once the one praying shows adequate.

AVOID MINDLESS REPETITION

The apostle Matthew, speaking on behalf of Jesus, warns us against empty and repetitive prayers. He cautions against *babbling like pagans*, which refers to mindless, repetitive, and insincere prayers. He discourages the idea that lengthy or repetitious prayers will necessarily gain God's favor. Instead, Jesus emphasizes the importance of heartfelt, genuine communication with God.

PRAY IN THE SPIRIT

These words occur in a passage where the apostle is indicating the contrast between the ungodly and the godly. The ungodly are mocking, speaking great swelling words, and walking after their ungodly lusts, while the righteous are building themselves up in their most holy faith, and keeping themselves in the love of God. The ungodly are showing the venom of their hearts by mourning and complaining, while the righteous are manifesting the new principle within them by "praying in the Holy Ghost." The ungodly man bears wormwood in his mouth, while the Christian's lips drop with the virgin honey of devotion. As the spider is said to find poison in the very flowers from which the bees suck honey, so do the wicked abuse to sin the selfsame mercies which the godly use to the glory of God. As far as light is removed from darkness,

and life from death, so far does a believer differ from the ungodly. Let us keep this contrast very vivid.[85]   –
Spurgeon

In addition to our persistence, we must pray in the Spirit. Ephesians 6:18 states: And pray in the Spirit on all occasions with all kinds of prayers and requests. Stay alert to your needs, and don't give up.

Prayer in the Spirit refers to praying under the guidance and influence of the Holy Spirit. It suggests that believers should not rely solely on their own understanding or words when praying but should seek the Spirit's leading and inspiration in their prayers.

> *In the same way, the Spirit helps us in our weakness. We do not know what we ought to pray for, but the Spirit himself intercedes for us through wordless groans. And he who searches our hearts knows the mind of the Spirit, because the Spirit intercedes for God's people in accordance with the will of God* (Romans 8:25-27).

QUALITY OVER QUANTITY

This passage encourages believers to focus on the quality of their prayers rather than the quantity or eloquence of words. God is interested in the sincerity, humility, and authenticity of our prayers rather than the length or complexity of our requests. *Hebrews 10:22 states: let us draw near to God with a sincere heart and with the full assurance that faith brings, having our hearts sprinkled to cleanse us from a guilty conscience and having our bodies washed with pure water.*

PRAYING IN THE WILL OF GOD

In James 5:16 the Spirit tells us: *The prayer of a righteous person is powerful and effective.* Believers must maintain a position of righteousness as they ask. Don't let your Satan dissuade you from your goal to have what you need.

TRUST IN GOD'S OMNISCIENCE

Jesus highlights the profound truth that God knows what we need before we ask Him. This position of understanding emphasizes the idea of

---

[85] Charles Spurgeon, Praying in the Holy Spirit, #719, Public Domain, spurgeongems.org. P. 1.

God's omniscience. He has complete knowledge and awareness of our circumstances, desires, and necessities. As a result, our prayers do not inform God but express our faith, trust, and dependence on Him.

RELATIONSHIP WITH GOD

Jesus underscores the idea of a personal and intimate relationship with God. Prayer is not merely a transactional request system, but a means of deepening our connection with the Trinity.

Spiritual Application:

Matthew 6:7 serves as a reminder of the importance of concise, sincere, and authentic communication with God in prayer. It discourages empty, repetitive, or showy prayers. We see His omniscience highlighted and the significance of an honest and heartfelt relationship with Him. The Savior's words encourage believers to approach prayer with humility, faith, and a desire to draw closer to God. We need God. We cannot survive the rigors of this world alone. His unfathomable understanding, willingness to help, and power to pull us through any circumstance are essential to our endurance.

Praying in concise language with purity and honest aspirations encourages believers to maintain a lifestyle of prayer led by the Holy Spirit, covers a wide range of topics, remains constant, and includes prayers for others. It stresses the importance of vigilance and caring for the spiritual needs of the Christian community.

Lessons within the Lesson:

List the thought-provoking verses or statements that spoke to you in this chapter.

Which statement may have the utmost impact on your prayer life?

How will your prayer life change because of this statement?

List the steps you will take to make the changes necessary to strengthen your prayer life.

26: PRAY BELIEVING GOD WILL ANSWER

Matthew 6:8

Opening Prayer:

My Savior and Lord, help me to trust in Your providential care. Give me the wisdom to align my prayers with Your will and to seek Your guidance in all my thoughts and actions. Convict me to be compliant with Your calling. May my prayers reflect the sincerity of my heart reaching into the depth of my faith. As I bring My concerns and needs before You, grant me the hope and peace that surpasses all understanding, knowing that You are a loving and attentive Father who desires the best for Your children. Teach me to be patient, Lord, and wait on Your perfect timing. You are in control. Your plans exceed mine. Your grace is boundless. Your love and compassion eternal. In Jesus' name, I pray. Amen!

Today's Bible Verse: **Matthew 6:8:**

Your Father knows the things you have need of before you ask Him.

Associated Scriptures:

And do not set your heart on what you will eat or drink; do not worry about it. For the pagan world runs after all such things, and your Father knows that you need them (Luke 12:29-30).

All my longings lie open before you, Lord; my sighing is not hidden from you (Psalm 38:9).

For the pagans run after all these things, and your

heavenly Father knows that you need them. (Matthew 6:32).

Correlative Quotes:

Prayer builds an altar and lays the sacrifice and the wood in order, and then love, like the priest, brings holy fire from heaven and sets the offering in a blaze. Faith is, as we have said, the root of grace, prayer is the lily's stalk, and love is the spotless flower. Faith sees the Savior, Prayer follows Him into the house, but love breaks the alabaster box of precious ointment and pours it on His head.[86] – Spurgeon

He (God) will have His children pray to Him, and He will link all His promised supplies to their petitions for them; thus encouraging us to draw near and keep near to Him, to talk and walk with Him to open our every case (need) to Him, and assure ourselves that thus asking we will receive, seeking we will find and knocking it will be opened to us.[87] – Jamieson, Fausset, and Brown

It is not the size of our prayers or the vocabulary of our prayers or the wordiness of our prayers that gets us a hearing with the Father. It is because we come to him in dependence upon the righteousness of Christ, casting ourselves upon his resources, and looking to him as our Father that grants our hearing. He "knows what you need before you ask Him," so your prayer does not need to be an attempt at manipulating the Father to give you what you want. For you cannot. It is rather a time to quiet your heart before him, to pour out your needs, and to cling to him in faithful dependence.[88] – Newton

Author's Notes:

INTRODUCTION

---

[86] Charles Spurgeon, Praying in the Holy Spirit, #79, Public Domain, Ibid., P. 1.

[87] Robert Jamieson, A.R. Fausset, David Brown, Commentary Critical and Explanatory on the Whole Bible, Vol. II, Public Domain, Ibid., P. 25.

[88] Dr. Phil Newton, No Hypocrisy, archive.southwoodsbc.org/sermons/matthew_06.01-08%2C16-18.php., Used by permission, Fair Use Authorization, Section 107, of the Copyright Law, P. 1.

The Sermon on the Mount is a central teaching of Jesus. He provides instructions on various aspects of the Christian life (6:1-4). He begins by explaining our responsibility to practice righteousness (vs. 1). After the instruction to meet the needs of the poor (Vs. 2), Jesus discusses prayer in detail.

In the verses preceding verse 8, Jesus addresses the practice of prayer (vs. 5). He contrasts the tendency of hypocrites to pray publicly with the more authentic and private approach His followers should adopt (vs. 6).

He then moves to His condemnation for the endless babbling of pagans who think they must entice their gods (figures sculpted by their own hands) using chants and voluminous amounts of words (vs. 7).

The theme of Matthew 6:8 is part of a broader context, emphasizing the sincerity and authenticity of a believer's prayers. It includes one of the more important theological concepts in the Holy Scriptures: His omniscience. God already knows what we need, what we will ask, and His response (Daniel 10:12). All this reflects an all-knowing nature of God. We refer to this divine attribute as His omniscience.

A LIVING FAITH

A disciple's relationship with God requires faith. Ephesians 2:8-9 explains this phenomenon: *For it is by grace you have been saved, through faith—and this is not from yourselves, it is the gift of God—not by works so that no one can boast.* To believe God will answer our prayer requires us to pray in faith.

SUBSTANTIATED BY SCRIPTURE

> *Therefore, since we have been justified through faith, we have peace with God through our Lord Jesus Christ, through whom we have gained access by faith into this grace in which we now stand. And we boast in the hope of the glory of God* (Romans 5:1-2).

Grace means unmerited favor. The unmerited favor of God (grace) came to us through faith, the gift of God (Ephesians 2:8-9), allowing us to receive eternal life through the gift of salvation. Therefore, both the grace and the faith came to us as gifts. We cannot boast.

APPROACH GOD WITH CONFIDENCE

Let us then approach God's throne of grace with confidence, so that we may receive mercy and find grace to help us in our time of need (Hebrews 4:16).

Hebrews 4:16 is a powerful encouragement for Christians to approach God with confidence. It reminds believers that they have direct access to God's grace and mercy through Jesus Christ. This verse underscores the idea that God is approachable and compassionate. He always stands ready to extend His help and favor to those who seek Him in faith. Knowing we have an option to turn to God as His children becomes a source of comfort and motivation for believers. We now, through faith, can turn to God in times of need. We are assured by His promises, knowing we will find the grace and mercy required to sustain us through difficult times of suffering.

DON'T FEAR

Do not be anxious about anything, but in every situation, by prayer and petition, with thanksgiving, present your requests to God (Philippians 4:6).

Philippians 4:6 offers a clear and practical approach to dealing with anxiety and worry. It instructs believers to replace fear with hope, love, and thanksgiving.

I have told you these things, so that in me you may have peace. In this world you will have trouble. But take heart! I have overcome the world (John 16:33).

By actively engaging with God in this way, believers can find peace and trust in God. He is attentive to their needs and cares for them. This verse underscores the importance of a healthy and active prayer life in maintaining emotional and spiritual well-being.

Cast all your anxiety on him because he cares for you (1 Peter 5:7).

ASK ANYTHING:

This is the confidence we have in approaching God: that if we ask anything according to his will, he hears us. And if we know that he hears us—whatever we ask—we know that we have what we asked of him. (1 John 5:14-15).

Through our relationship with God, we have confidence in approaching Him. Our assurance is rooted in the believer's relationship with God through faith in Jesus Christ.

There is therefore now no condemnation to those who are in Christ Jesus, who do not walk according to the flesh, but according to the Spirit. (Romans 8:1, NKJV).

First, we must ask according to God's will. This action suggests that believers can come before God, knowing He is approachable and attentive to their prayers. Hebrews 10:19 tells us the blood of Christ paves the way to enter the presence of God when the Spirit of God says: *Therefore, brothers and sisters, since we have confidence to enter the Most Holy Place by the blood of Jesus.*

Praying according to His will highlights the need for submission and alignment with God's plan (Jeremiah 29:11). To be in the Lord's will, we must submit to Him. Compliance acknowledges how God's wisdom surpasses human understanding (Job 11:7-12), and His will is ultimately for the believer's good (Philippians 2:13).

GOD HEARS US (1 John 5:14)

John assures believers that when they pray by God's will, He hears their prayers (Colossians 1:9). This acknowledgment of God's attentiveness underscores His relational nature and His desire to engage with His children through prayer.

PRAY THROUGH RIGHTEOUSNESS: (1 John 5:14)

The Lord is far from the wicked, but he hears the prayer of the righteous (Proverbs 15:29).

John further declares if believers know that God hears their prayers (because they are living in obedience), they can be confident in receiving what they have asked for. This confidence reflects the believer's faith in God's faithfulness. His commitment to provide for our needs mirrors the harmony between our essentials and His purpose.

FAITH AND RELATIONSHIP:

The Matthew 6:8 passage emphasizes the importance of faith and the believer's relationship with God through Christ. Trusting God to answer our prayers finds its anchor in the believer's trust in God's character and purpose. Live firm in your commitment to Him.

Spiritual Application:

In summary, Matthew 6:8 underscores the confidence believers can have when approaching God in prayer. It emphasizes the importance of praying in alignment with God's will and the assurance that God hears and answers their prayers. This passage highlights the relational and faith-based nature prayer can bring to the Christian's life.

Within the context of the Sermon on the Mount, we see a vast array of commands and promises. Matthew 6:8 serves us as an encouragement from Jesus to approach prayer with authenticity and sincerity. It emphasizes God's omniscience and His role as a loving Father who cares deeply for His children. This verse invites believers to cultivate a genuine and continuing relationship with God through prayer rather than engaging in empty religious rituals.

God invites all to believe (John 3:16). He explains how we attain eternal life (Romans 10:9-10). Finally, He promises to fulfill the needs of those who believe and continue to live in His will by making Jesus the Lord of their lives. Faith never seems easy, but it brings great rewards..

Lessons within the Lesson:

List the thought-provoking verses or statements that spoke to you in this chapter.

Which statement may have the utmost impact on your prayer life?

How will your prayer life change because of this statement?

List the steps you will take to make the changes necessary to strengthen your prayer life.

27: PRAYING WITH THANKSGIVING

Ephesians 5:17-20

Opening Prayer:

O Lord, I approach Your throne with humility. I am in awe of Your power to save and Your willingness to comfort those who love You. I seek wisdom and understanding. I thank You for the guidance and clarity Your Word provides. Motivate me to apply it in my words and works. Grant me the wisdom to understand Your will in every area of my life. Embolden me to be wise in my decision-making. Allow me to see the life path You have laid out before me. Remind me continually to recognize the supremacy of Your plans. They are far greater than mine.

I thank you for the precious gift of time you have given me. I pray for the continued opportunity to serve You and to show Your love to others. Convict me in the times when I am careless. You've granted us the knowledge of the ancients as a guide. Encourage me to use them to bring glory to Your name.

Direct me through the Holy Spirit, Lord. Continually fill me with gratitude and joy. Help me to overflow with praise, singing songs to You in my heart, giving thanks for all the blessings You have bestowed upon me. Glorious, Glorious is Your name, a name above all names. It is in Your name, Lord, I pray. Amen!

Today's Bible Verse: Ephesians 5:17-20

Be filled with the Spirit, speaking to one another with psalms, hymns, and songs from the Spirit. Sing and make music from your heart to the Lord, always giving thanks to God the Father for everything, in the name of our Lord Jesus Christ.

Associated Scriptures:

Give thanks in all circumstances; for this is the will of God in Christ Jesus for you (1 Thessalonians 5:18, ESV).

Oh give thanks to the Lord, for he is good, for his steadfast love endures forever! (Psalm 107:1, ESV).

And let the peace of Christ rule in your hearts, to which indeed you were called in one body. And be thankful (Colossians 3:15).

Correlative Quotes:

In the position of our text are bid to speak to themselves and one another in psalms and hymns and spiritual songs, singing and making melody in their hearts to the Lord. If they cannot be always singing they are always to maintain the spirit of song. If they must of necessity desist at intervals from outward expressions of praise, they ought never to refrain from inwardly giving thanks. The apostle having touched upon the act of singing in public worship, here points out the essential part of it, which lies not in classic music and thrilling harmonies, but in the melody of the heart. Thanksgiving is the soul of all acceptable singing.[89] – Spurgeon

"Be filled with the Spirit" is God's command, and He expects us to obey. The command is plural, so it applies to all Christians and not just to a select few. The verb is in the present tense— "keep on being filled"—so it is an experience we should enjoy constantly and not just on special occasions. And the verb is passive. We do not fill ourselves but permit the Spirit to fill us.[90] – Wiersbe

Another evidence of being filled with the Spirit is an attitude of thankfulness. We note in the Book of Psalms a great amount

---

[89] Charles Spurgeon, Always, And For All Things, Public Domain, spurgeongems.org., P. 1.
[90] Warren Wiersbe, The Wiersbe Bible Commentary: N. T., Ibid., P. 615.

of thanksgiving and praise to God. And it is on a high level. We don't have enough of that among believers today. We should all say, *Praise the Lord and thanks be to God for his unspeakable gift.* Can we say that from the heart? It is no good unless it comes from the heart. The filling of the Holy Spirit produces a life of thankfulness so that we can honestly thank God for all things.[91] – McGee

Author's Notes:

INTRODUCTION

Praying to God with thanksgiving brings joy to God and happiness and satisfaction to His children. A thankful heart marks the appreciation to God for the blessings, provisions, and experiences in the Christian life. This practice addresses several critical purposes on a personal and spiritual level. A grateful heart represents a significant action in our spiritual journey. It can transform our perspective, strengthen our faith, and deepen our relationship with our Heavenly Father. As we proceed in this chapter, reflect upon the profound wisdom found in Ephesians 5:20 and seek to incorporate the reasons for thankfulness into our daily lives.

GRATITUDE AND HUMILITY:

> *Therefore, by Him let us continually offer the sacrifice of praise to God, that is, the fruit of our lips, giving thanks to His name. But do not forget to do good and to share* (with others (NIV), *for with such sacrifices God is well pleased* (Hebrews 13:15-16, NKJV).

When we pray from the heart with a deep need and humble spirit, we foster humility by recognizing the good things God has provided. We also show our appreciation for God's generosity. It encourages individuals to acknowledge their dependence on a higher power and appreciate the abundance of blessings they have received. Psalm 9:1-2 substantiates this thought when it reveals the heart of the psalmist: *I will give thanks to you, Lord, with all my heart; I will tell of all your wonderful deeds. I will be glad and rejoice in you; I will sing the praises of your name, O Most High.*

---

[91] J. Vernon McGee, Through the Bible with J. Vernon McGee, Vol. V, 1 Corinthians-Revelation., Ibid. P. 266.

POSITIVE OUTLOOK

> *And whatever you do, whether in word or deed, do it all in the name of the Lord Jesus, giving thanks to God the Father through him* (Colossians 3:17).

Colossians 3:17 emphasizes the importance of a prayerful and God-centered approach to life. It calls us to integrate prayer into every aspect of our existence, seeking to align our actions and words with the teachings and character of Jesus Christ while maintaining an attitude of gratitude towards God the Father. This approach leads to a more purposeful and spiritually enriched life.

Prayers of thanksgiving will help Christians shift their focus from problems and challenges to the positive aspects of life. This attitude of faith can lead to a more confident and optimistic outlook, even in the face of overwhelming difficulties.

Assurance of our position in God will accelerate the certainty found in belief and release the apprehension leading to discouragement. Success through Christ encourages us to continue a positive attitude toward a shared love relationship with Him.

STRENGTHENING OUR RELATIONSHIP WITH GOD:

> *The end of all things is near. Therefore, be alert and of sober mind so that you may pray. Above all, love each other deeply, because love covers over a multitude of sins. Offer hospitality to one another without grumbling. Each of you should use whatever gift you have received to serve others, as faithful stewards of God's grace in its various forms* (1 Peter 4:7-10).

Thanking God in prayer deepens the connection with Him and others. Acknowledgment of His involvement in the lives of the saved, His care about all His sons and daughters' well-being, and finally, His response to needs and expressions of gratitude strengthen our ongoing earthly and heavenly lovefest.

CONTENTMENT:

> *But godliness with contentment is great gain. For we brought nothing into the world, and we can take nothing*

*out of it. But if we have food and clothing, we will be
content with that* (1 Timothy 6:6-8).

Expressing gratitude through prayer can lead to a sense of contentment and satisfaction. We came to this world wearing only our skin. When we leave, even our covering will return to dust. Everything we have is a gift from God. Be content with what He has provided for you. By acknowledging and being thankful for what one has, there's less focus on what is lacking, leading to greater contentment and happiness.

PRAISE AND WORSHIP:

> *You are holy, Enthroned in the praises of Israel* (Psalm
> 22:3, NKJV).

God loves to hear us worship Him. Giving honor and glory to the Creator represents our most impressive act of worship. Prayers of thanksgiving often include praise and adoration for God's character, love, and faithfulness. It provides an opportunity to lift God's name and attributes, acknowledging His goodness and love for His children.

COMMUNITY AND SHARING:

> *And let us consider how we may spur one another on
> toward love and good deeds, not giving up meeting
> together, as some are in the habit of doing, but
> encouraging one another—and all the more as you see
> the Day approaching* (Hebrews 10:24-25.

A relationship with others is spiritual, not physical. When in assembly, we should focus on all and not just the few. We should share prayers of thanksgiving in community or in public worship settings. This communal practice allows believers to celebrate together, fostering a sense of unity and shared gratitude.

PERSONAL GROWTH:

> *But grow in the grace and knowledge of our Lord and
> Savior Jesus Christ. To him be glory both now and
> forever! Amen* (2 Peter 3:18).

The Spirit demands that we grow spiritually. Growth brings us closer to God and strengthens our relationship with His Spirit and other

Christians. Praying with thanksgiving encourages personal growth by emphasizing the importance of recognizing and appreciating the positive aspects of life. This practice contributes to spiritual and emotional development..

COPING WITH CHALLENGES:

> *Instruct the wise and they will be wiser still; teach the righteous and they will add to their learning* (Proverbs 9:9, NKJV).

Righteousness remains the number one issue for all Christianity. Nothing happens without obedience. The three key steps to living a life of conformity to the Spirit include salvation from God, continued fellowship with God, and repentance when we err against God. All three have a foundation of prayer. We pray to receive salvation (Romans 10:9-10). We pray to maintain fellowship (Galatians 5:16). Finally, we repent when we transgress (1 John 1:8).

Spiritual Application:

Praying with thanksgiving is a valuable spiritual discipline that enriches one's relationship with God and contributes to overall well-being and a positive attitude. It is a practice that can be incorporated into daily routines, helping individuals maintain a grateful and appreciative mindset. Practice unconditional love for God and for others and watch your prayer life change for the better.

Lessons within the Lesson:

List the thought-provoking verses or statements that spoke to you in this chapter.

Which statement may have the utmost impact on your prayer life?

How will your prayer life change because of this statement?

List the steps you will take to make the changes necessary to strengthen your prayer life.

28. QUESTION #4: WHEN DO WE PRAY?

1 Thessalonians 5:17

Opening Prayer:

O Lord, I recognize that I cannot confine prayer to a specific time or place. It is a constant conversation with You, my loving Father. I thank You for the privilege of communing with You in moments of quiet reflection and amid our daily routines. Help me, O Lord, to cultivate a spirit of unceasing prayer in my life. Teach me to make my thoughts, words, and actions one with Your will. Guide my prayers with Your wisdom. Embrace me with Your love so I might better love You and others. In personal moments of joy, I thank You. Thank You for Your unconditional love and grace. In the Savior's name, I pray. Amen.**Today's Bible Verse**: **1 Thessalonians 5:17**

Pray without ceasing.

Associated Scriptures:

Then He spoke a parable to them, that men always ought to pray and not lose heart (Luke 18:1).

Evening, morning and noon I cry out in distress, and He hears my voice (Psalm 55:17).

Watch and pray so that you will not fall into temptation. The spirit is willing, but the flesh is weak (Matthew 26:41).

Correlative Quotes:

Your knee may be bent before the altar of God, though they are stained through many a fall into sin. Though it is many years since you ever thought of praying, yet you may pray. Though, perhaps, you have even denied that there is a God, still you may pray. Though you have ridiculed the very notion of prayer, you may pray. God does not refuse to you the permission to come to His mercy seat. Though you have committed every crime in the catalog of sin, you may pray. And though you have gone on in those crimes and involved yourself yet more and more deeply in iniquity, you may pray. Though you are within a few days of death and of damnation, unless the grace of God shall visit you, yet you may pray.[92] – Spurgeon

Continual prayer is not prayer that prevails without any interruption, but prayer that continues whenever possible. The adverb for continually was used in Greek of a hacking cough. Paul was speaking of maintaining continuous fellowship with God as much as possible in the midst of daily living in which concentration is frequently broken.[93] – Walvoord and Zuck

This has to do with an attitude of prayer. I don't think this means that one is to stay on his knees all the time. But it means to pray regularly and be consistently in the attitude of prayer.[94]   – McGee

Author's Notes:

INTRODUCTION

Prayer is a struggle for most believers. We want to talk to God, but the many distractions of life get in the way. Many of those distractions should be the subject of our prayers. However, we often don't think about praying when we have the greatest need.

According to a Pew research study completed in 2023, 60% of Christians pray at least once a day, 17% pray weekly, 5% pray monthly,

---

[92] Charles Spurgeon, When Should We Pray?, Message # 2591., spurgeongems.org., P. 1.
[93] John Walvoord and Roy B. Zuck, The Bible Knowledge Commentary, Ibid., Pp. 708-9.
[94] J. Vernon McGee, Through the Bible with J. Vernon McGee, Vol. V, Ibid., P.404.

and 18% seldom or never pray.[95] – Pew Research

Since prayer is fundamental to the Christian experience, we should talk to God continually. He doesn't mind if we talk to Him regularly.

PRAYER IS TALKING WITH GOD.

> *Then you will call on me and come and pray to me, and I will listen to you. You will seek me and find me when you seek me with all your heart. I will be found by you (Jeremiah 29:12-14a).*

Cursing doesn't count. Using God's name outside of direct communication should never happen with His disciples since it is demeaning to His character.

I have played golf often in my lifetime. Many golfers seem to hold God accountable for every terrible shot they make and take personal credit for all of the good ones. When someone yells God's name, usually followed by another common expletive, I may ask: Where? I didn't see Him! I have received some strange looks over the years. However, those who are guilty of profanity usually ignore me. I have never ended up wearing one of their golf clubs and will probably quit asking if it occurs.

While the passages in this section of the book provides guidance on when to pray, it is essential to remember that prayer is a personal and intimate connection with God.

ANY TIME, ANY PLACE

> *I love those who love me, and those who seek me find me (Proverbs 8:17).*

Believers can pray anytime and they may express their thoughts, emotions, and needs to their Heavenly Father. Ultimately, the Bible encourages a continuous and heartfelt relationship with God through prayer. Our Bible verse for today sets a precedent when Paul writes in 1 Thessalonians chapter 5 verse 17: Pray without ceasing. This verse isn't a suggestion. It is a command.

Anytime is the appropriate time to talk to God. He is there all the

---

[95] Pew Research, Frequency of Prayer Among Christians, pewresearch.org/religion/religious-landscape-study/christians/christian/frequency-of-prayer/, P. 1.

time. However, like everything else in life, we forget. Therefore, it becomes imperative to establish a habit of prayer. Scheduling times to pray and putting them on our phones or the calendar will be a good reminder.

Once we have established the specific times we would like to pray, it would be wise to set an alarm to remind us. Cell phones allow us to set alarms by the number of desired times during the day and the frequency to remind us. The phone allows us to make these commitments as a reminder.

REWARD FOR FAITH AND DEVOTION: (Vss. 1-3).

> *It pleased Darius to appoint 120 satraps to rule throughout the kingdom, with three administrators over them, one of whom was Daniel. The satraps were made accountable to them so that the king might not suffer loss. Now Daniel so distinguished himself among the administrators and the satraps by his exceptional qualities that the king planned to set him over the whole kingdom.*

Daniel displayed an unwavering faith and devotion to his God. Due to these traits, God blessed Daniel with knowledge and understanding. Because of Daniel's wisdom, the king committed to placing the Israeli immigrant over the entire kingdom.

JEALOUSY AND CONSPIRACY: (Vss. 4-9).

> *Now, Your Majesty, issue the decree and put it in writing so that it cannot be altered—in accordance with the law of the Medes and Persians, which cannot be repealed. So King Darius put the decree in writing (7-9).*

King Darius' decision infuriated the royal administrators, prefects, satraps, advisers, and governors. In retaliation, they convinced King Darius to pass a law prohibiting anyone from praying to someone other than the King. Despite the ruling from King Darius, Daniel continued to practice His prayerful worship of the one true God.

WHEN GOD COMES CALLING

> *Now when Daniel learned that the decree had been published, he went home to his upstairs room where the*

144

windows opened toward Jerusalem. Three times a day
he got down on his knees and prayed, giving thanks to
his God, just as he had done before (Daniel 6:10).

Daniel, a victim of the Israeli Babylonian diaspora, after hearing the King's command to pray only for the magistrate himself, went to his room and prayed to God according to His habit of praying three times a day. Despite being a high-ranking official in the Persian government, he remains steadfast in his worship of Yahweh and refuses to compromise his religious beliefs. Daniel considered God's love more important than Man's rules.

THE KINGS DILEMMA (Verses. 11-12).

Then these men went as a group and found Daniel
praying and asking God for help. So they went to the
king and spoke to him about his royal decree: The king
answered, The decree stands—in accordance with the
law of the Medes and Persians, which cannot be
repealed.

The administrators, prefects, satraps, advisers, and governors used Daniel's faithfulness to his God as a pretext to have him removed from his position and ultimately cast into the lion's den. King Darius is caught in a moral dilemma. He admires Daniel and does not want to see him harmed, but he is bound by the law he signed. It decrees that anyone who prays to any god or man other than the king during a specific period should be thrown into the lion's den.

THE KINGS REGRET AND SORROW (Verses. 13-18).

When the king heard this, he was greatly distressed; he
was determined to rescue Daniel and made every effort
until sundown to save him (14).

This prideful action established a conflict between the King Darius' human authority and God's divine authority. Who do you think is going to win that battle of wills?

DIVINE PROTECTION: (Verses 18-23)

The officials throw Daniel into the lion's den. They secure a stone over the opening. The king spends a sleepless night. In the morning, he finds Daniel unharmed because God has protected him.

ANSWERED PRAYER IMPACTS OTHERS' LIVES

King Darius praises the God of Daniel, issues a new decree commanding reverence for Daniel's God, and promotes Daniel to an even higher position in the kingdom. The jealous officials who plotted against Daniel are thrown into the lion's den and meet their demise.

Spiritual Application:

Daniel chapter 6 has become a powerful and inspirational narrative cherished by believers over the centuries. These few verses of dedication to right and defying wrong illustrate the triumph found in prayer, faith, and divine intervention. The lives of those who remain steadfast in their devotion to God have changed radically. When placed in positions of enormous pressure, this passage of scripture has been a catalyst to change the lives and hearts of Christians everywhere.

This text underscores the importance of faith and loyalty to God, even when confronted with adversity and persecution. This chapter demonstrates God's faithfulness in protecting those who trust in Him.

It also serves as a lesson about the consequences of jealousy and deceit. It highlights the tension between human authority and divine authority, ultimately emphasizing the supremacy of God.

We must reach out to God in prayer when life's circumstances seem overwhelming with no end in sight. God knows and controls the future. Prayers such as Daniel's bring hope when all hope seems lost.

Lessons within the Lesson:

List the thought-provoking verses or statements that spoke to you in this chapter.

Which statement may have the utmost impact on your prayer life?

How will your prayer life change because of this statement?

List the steps you will take to make the changes necessary to strengthen your prayer life.

29: LEAD BY THE SPIRIT

2 Corinthians 3:18

Opening Prayer:

Heavenly Father, I come before you with a heart filled with gratitude for Your constant presence in my lives. We are continually directed and fulfilled by Your Spirit. You are my Rock and our Refuge, my ever-present help in times of trouble. Today, I lift our hearts in prayer, seeking Your guidance and strength in every situation. Direct me through Your Spirit to keep me on the track to a Spirit-led life in Christ. Lord, You are the One who equips me with wisdom and discernment. I ask for Your guidance to make wise decisions and to be proactive in preparing for the challenges and uncertainties that lie ahead. Support me as I attempt to live as a good steward of the resources and abilities You have given me. Grant me the wisdom to prepare not only for our well-being but also for the welfare of others. Open my eyes to the needs of those around me. Make me an instrument of Your love and compassion. Direct me to Your Word for guidance and comfort during times of confusion. Fill me with Your peace that surpasses all understanding, anchoring our hearts in Your unchanging love. Prepare me for every life situation, I know I am never alone. In Jesus' name, we pray. Amen!

Today's Bible Verse: 2 Corinthians 3:18

And we all, who with unveiled faces contemplate the Lord's glory, are being transformed into his image with ever-increasing glory, which comes from the Lord, who is the Spirit.

Ephesians 2:18-20.

For through Him we both have access to the Father by one Spirit. Consequently, you are no longer foreigners and strangers, but fellow citizens with God's people and also members of his household, built on the foundation of the apostles and prophets, with Christ Jesus Himself as the chief cornerstone.

Associated Scriptures:

This is what we speak, not in words taught us by human wisdom but in words taught by the Spirit, explaining spiritual realities with Spirit-taught words (1 Corinthians 2:13).

I urge you, brothers, by our Lord Jesus Christ and by the love of the Spirit, to join me in my struggle by praying to God for me (Romans 15:30-31).

But you, dear friends, by building yourselves up in your most holy faith and praying in the Holy Spirit (Jude 1:20).

Correlative Quotes:

How greatly we ought to value the Holy Spirit. When our perplexed spirit is so befogged and beclouded that it cannot see its own need and cannot find out the appropriate promise in the Scriptures, the Spirit of God comes in and teaches us all things and brings all things to our remembrance whatsoever our Lord has told us. He guides us in prayer and thus He helps our infirmity. He directs the mind to the special subject of prayer. He dwells within us as a Counselor and points out to us what it is we should seek at the hands of God. At such times we should thank God for direction and give our desire a clear road. The Holy Spirit is granting us inward direction as to how we should order our petitions before the throne of grace and we may now reckon upon success in our pleadings.[96] – Spurgeon

And only through him do We both have access. The

---

[96] Charles Spurgeon, The Holy Spirit's Intercession, Message # 1532, spurgeongems.org., Pp. 2-3.

continuous, common, and unhindered approach to God. Through Christ all believers can come boldly into his grace (Hebrews 4:16) By one spirit. Our access to the Father is through the Son and by the Holy Spirit all three persons of the Trinity share in the total work of salvation.[97] – Roustio

Anyone believer has as much access to God as any other believer. People ask me why I didn't have a select few pray for me when I had a bout with cancer. Why didn't I ask everyone to pray? I did it because I believe in the priesthood of believers, that is, all believers have access to him.[98]   – McGee

Author's Notes:

INTRODUCTION

Romans 8:26-27 states: *In the same way, the Spirit helps us in our weakness. We do not know what we ought to pray for, but the Spirit himself intercedes for us through wordless groans. And he who searches our hearts knows the mind of the Spirit because the Spirit intercedes for God's people in accordance with the will of God.*

The statement, *we pray as we are led by the Spirit,* sums up how our prayers should be guided by the Holy Spirit. It aligns with the biblical concept of being led by the Spirit in our Christian walk.

Paul explains in Galatians 5:16-18: *So I say, live by the Spirit, and you will not gratify the desires of the sinful nature. For the sinful nature desires what is contrary to the Spirit, and the Spirit what is contrary to the sinful nature. They are in conflict with each other, so that you do not do what you want. But if you are led by the Spirit, you are not under law.*

These passages emphasize the Holy Spirit's role in prayer in our lives, especially His mission in our prayer lives. It suggests there are times when we may not know how to pray effectively, but the Spirit intercedes on our behalf, aligning our prayers with the will of God. The Spirit leads us into the Truth. The Truth describes God's Word. Through prayer and the Word

---

[97] Edward R. Roustio, Liberty Bible Commentary, published by Old Gospel Hour, Nashville, Tenn. P. 2501, Used by permission, Fair Use Authorization, Section 107, of the Copyright Law, P. 2412.

[98] J. Vernon McGee, Through the Bible with J. Vernon McGee, Vol. V Ibid., P. 240.

we are being led to the throne of God by His Spirit. Transformation (sanctification) begins with salvation and ends with glorification. We will all receive perfection in the presence of God.

THREE STEPS TO PERFECTION

> And those he predestined, he also called; those he called, he also **justified**; those he **justified**, he also **glorified** (Romans 8:30).

The process of becoming perfect in the eyes of God involves three words. They are justification (salvation), sanctification (transformation), and glorification (perfection).

Justification (salvation) is past tense. It refers to our position in Christ Jesus (Romas 51). Justification, or being saved, manifests itself through God's grace, by faith alone (Ephesians 2:8-9).

Sanctification happens in the present and is ongoing.

> To sanctify an object means to wash, cleanse, consecrate or set it aside for a special purpose. Sanctification is a Christian teaching about how God transforms a person, making them fit for a holy purpose. Sanctification includes a change of heart, a desire to love God and other people. It includes a change of mind, it means seeing the world from an honest perspective.[99]
> – Campus Crusade for Christ

Positional sanctification takes place at salvation. We are positionally pure in the eyes of God. Progressive Sanctification is ongoing.

1 Thessalonians 5:23a says, "*May God himself, the God of peace, sanctify you through and through.*" Philippians 1:6 explains that, "*being confident of this, that he who began a good work in you will carry it on to completion until the day of Christ Jesus.*" Sanctification is the state of being holy (positional), but it is also the process of becoming holy (progressive).

Unlike justification, Sanctification represents the progressive action of transformation. Our goal involves becoming more like Christ. 2 Corinthians 3:18 teaches: *And we all, who with unveiled faces contemplate the Lord's glory, are being transformed into His image with ever-increasing*

---

[99] Campus Crusade for Christ, What is Sanctification and how does it work.

glory, which comes from the Lord, who is the Spirit.

The final act in our desire to become perfect comes through glorification. Glorification is in the future. The Bible describes the last step as permanent. We expect to be like Christ. Paul describes this occurrence in 2 Timothy 4:8 when he writes (under the inspiration of the Holy Spirit): *Now there is in store for me the crown of righteousness, which the Lord, the righteous Judge, will award to me on that day—and not only to me but also to all who have longed for his appearing.*

TRANSFORMED BY THE SPIRIT

> *Do not conform any longer to the pattern of this world, but be transformed by the renewing of your mind. Then you will be able to test and approve what God's will is — his good, pleasing and perfect will* (Romans 12:1-2).

UNVEILED FACES:

The passage begins by referring to *unveiled faces*. In the context of this chapter, Paul contrasts the Old Covenant with the New Covenant. In the Old Covenant, Moses veiled his face after encountering God's glory, symbolizing the temporary and veiled nature of God's revelation. In contrast, believers in the New Covenant can now approach God with unveiled faces, indicating direct and unhindered access to God's presence through Christ.

CONTEMPLATING THE LORD'S GLORY:

Secondly, With our eyes no longer blindfolded by sin's blinding darkness We now behold *the Lord's glory*. This Christ-centered vision of the Word of God and the interpretation of His Spirit implies a deep, focused, and reflective view of the glory of God revealed in Christ. As His followers meditate on Christ and His redemptive work, they are transformed by the profound truths they behold.

TRANSFORMATION INTO HIS IMAGE:

In this verse, seekers see the central Truth, the essence of transformation. Experiencing ongoing sanctification emphasizes a new knowledge of God's glory and how to achieve it. As a result, the saved are becoming transformed into His image. This transformation does not represent a superficial change but a complete inner and spiritual rebirth.

151

Our spirit, dead in Adam, now comes alive in Christ (John 3:1-5 and 1 Corinthians 15:22), and believers become more like Christ in character, attitude, and actions.

EVER-INCREASING GLORY:

This Scripture pictures transformation, unlike salvation, as a multifaceted event with an ongoing process. Believers experience *ever-increasing glory*. This statement confirms the transforming of the Spirit as a continuous and progressive growth in the likeness of Christ. This process is directed and empowered by the Holy Spirit.

SOURCE OF TRANSFORMATION:

The verse also underscores the crucial role of the Holy Spirit in the process of sanctification and spiritual growth. The Holy Spirit is the agent of transformation, working within believers to conform them to the image of Christ. Colossians 1:27 confirms this truth when the apostle writes: *To them God has chosen to make known among the Gentiles the glorious riches of this mystery, which is Christ in you, the hope of glory.*

REFLECTING GOD'S GLORY:

In 2 Corinthians 3:18, the purpose of the believer's transformation comes to life. Paul wants us to see the reflective radiance of God's glory. As believers become more like Christ, they manifest God's character and attributes to the world, drawing others to Him. This verse beautifully reminds us of the work of the Holy Spirit in the lives of believers. It encourages us to fix our gaze on the glory of the Lord, knowing that as we do, we are continually changing to reflect His image more fully and to bring honor and glory to His name.

CONFLICT BETWEEN FLESH AND SPIRIT:

> But each one is tempted when he is drawn away by his own desires and enticed. Then, when desire has conceived, it gives birth to sin; and sin, when it is full-grown, brings forth death (James 1:14-15).

Paul highlights the inherent conflict between the flesh and the Spirit. These two forces are in opposition to each other. Our ungodly desires pull us toward self-indulgence, while the Spirit prompts believers toward righteousness, holiness, and love.

FREEDOM FROM THE DESIRES OF THE FLESH:

Walking by the Spirit results in victory over the desires of the flesh. The urging of self-desires refers to sinful and self-centered inclinations. These actions and reactions are contrary to God's will. By yielding to the Spirit, believers can resist and overcome these antigod desires.

WALKING BY THE SPIRIT:

> But if we walk in the light, as he is in the light, we have fellowship with one another, and the blood of Jesus, his Son, purifies us from all sin (1 John 1:7).

To walk in the light means to live in God's Word, the Bible. The Spirit interprets His Word. Paul encourages believers to walk by the Spirit. This way of life involves His guidance, prompting, and empowerment. The Spirit is the source of all life. He also directs us. He calls us to a life of obedience to His will, allowing the Spirit to lead and direct our actions.

FREEDOM FROM THE LAW:

> What then? Shall we sin because we are not under the law but under grace? By no means! (Romans 6:15).

Does our freedom from the law allow us to sin? This new liberty under grace does not keep us from sin! The apostle is emphatic about this truth. When we empower the Spirit to lead, we no longer answer to the law. This truth underscores the idea that the law, while essential in revealing His standards and the sinfulness of humanity, cannot save or sanctify. The transformative work of the Holy Spirit enables obedient believers to ignore the law's controlling effect.

THE FRUIT OF THE SPIRIT:

Galatians 5:22-23 describes the fruit of the Spirit, which includes love, joy, peace, patience, kindness, goodness, faithfulness, gentleness, and self-control. These qualities characterize the life of believers when they let the Spirit lead.

Galatians 5:16-18 emphasizes the need for believers to live in step with the Holy Spirit. God's children must allow the Spirit to guide and empower them. By doing so, they can overcome the desires of the flesh

These passages underscore the importance of an ongoing

relationship with the Spirit, producing godly character and conduct in the lives of believers.

Walking with the Spirit underscores the importance of believers living in harmony with the Spirit. When we walk in step with the Spirit, He is more likely to answer our prayers since they align with God's purposes and desires.

PRAYING IN THE SPIRIT

> *And pray in the Spirit on all occasions with all kinds of prayers and requests. With this in mind, be alert and always keep on praying for all the Lord's people* (Ephesians 6:18).

In the verse from Ephesians, we are encouraged to pray "in the Spirit" at all times and in various ways. Verse 18 suggests that the Spirit can guide and inspire our prayers, making them more effective since they are according to God's will.

DECERNING GOD'S ROLE IN PRAYER

> *For who knows a person's thoughts except their own spirit within them? In the same way, no one knows the thoughts of God except the Spirit of God. What we have received is not the spirit of the world, but the Spirit who is from God so that we may understand what God has freely given us.* (1 Corinthians 2:11-12).

This passage highlights the Holy Spirit's role in helping believers understand and discern God's wisdom and blessings. This understanding can influence the content and direction of our prayers.

We align with the biblical teachings regarding the Holy Spirit's involvement in our prayer life when our prayers agree with the will of God. It emphasizes the importance of seeking the guidance and inspiration of the Holy Spirit in our prayers, trusting that the Spirit intercedes for us and orients our prayers with God's will.

It also underscores the need for believers to maintain a close and obedient relationship with the Spirit to ensure our prayers are in harmony with God's will and purposes.

Since we live by the Spirit, let us keep in step with the Spirit (Galatians 5:25).

The Spirit of God plays a significant and transformative role in the prayer life of believers. He provides guidance and wisdom in our prayers. The Spirit can reveal God's will, enlighten our understanding, and help us discern the right course of action. This guidance is valuable when we face complex decisions or challenging circumstances.

The Holy Spirit empowers us to pray boldly and fervently. It gives us the confidence to approach God's throne of grace with assurance and trust. Through the Spirit's empowerment, we can pray with faith, believing God can answer our petitions.

The Spirit of God can open our spiritual eyes and ears, enabling us to see and understand spiritual realities. This insight allows us to pray with a deeper understanding of God's kingdom, His purposes, and the spiritual battles that may be at play in our lives.

God's Spirit helps us discern the difference between our desires and His will. This discernment enables us to align our prayers with His plans and prevents us from praying selfishly or outside His purposes.

The Holy Spirit equips us for spiritual warfare by helping us pray against the forces of darkness. It provides us with the spiritual armor (Ephesians 6:10-18) needed to stand firm in prayer and resist the enemy.

Spiritual Application:

For Moses the glory eventually faded away, but under the new covenant the believer is changed into the same image. Paul has already established that quotation marks as we have born the image of the earthly, we will also bear the image of the heavenly end quotation marks 2 Corinthians 15:49. The apostle John says that ultimately we will be just like Christ because quotes we shall see him as he is 1 John 3:2. Even as by the spirit of the Lord. This transformation takes place by the abiding presence of the spirit of God.[100] – Mitchell

---

[100] Daniel Mitchell, Liberty Bible Commentary, The Old-Time Gospel Hour, Lynchburg, Virginia,

The Spirit of God plays a multifaceted role in our prayers, guiding, empowering, and transforming us as we seek to communicate with God. By relying on the Spirit's leading and intercession, our prayers become more aligned with God's will and more effective in our spiritual journey.

The Spirit can foster unity among believers and inspire corporate prayer. It moves individuals to intercede for one another, their communities, and the world.

Such unified prayer can have a powerful impact on the church and society. Praying in the Spirit deepens our relationship with God. It allows us to commune with God, fostering intimacy and a sense of God's presence in our lives.

Through prayer in the Spirit, the Holy Spirit can transform our hearts and minds, conforming us more closely to the image of Christ. This process of sanctification impacts the content and character of our prayers.

Lessons within the Lesson:

List the thought-provoking verses or statements that spoke to you in this chapter.

Which statement may have the utmost impact on your prayer life?

How will your prayer life change because of this statement?

List the steps you will take to make the changes necessary to strengthen your prayer life.

30: TIMING IN PRAYER

Psalm 55:16-19

Opening Prayer:

Our God and Father, creator of all in existence, I come to You just now asking for Your help. Lord, I am grateful for Your presence in my life, the good, the bad, the ugly. Your continuous availability brings assurance, regardless of the time or circumstance, and provides comfort.

In the evening, when the day's challenges weigh heavy on my heart, I cry out to You, seeking Your understanding and the peace You have promised in Romans 5:1. Thank You for being the source of solace in our times of distress.

In the morning, as a new day dawns with its uncertainties and opportunities, I lift my voice to You. Guide my steps this another day, Lord, and grant me wisdom as I navigate the path before me.

At noon, I pause to seek witness of Your love. Amid the daily routine, help me remember Your presence. You listen to my every concern and provide strength for my daily journey.

We acknowledge, O Lord, Your faithfulness. You hear our prayers, and You respond with love and grace. Your understanding knows no bounds, and Your mercy has no end. For it is in the name of Your Son, Jesus Christ, who intercedes for us, we pray. Amen.

Today's Bible Verse: Psalm 55:16-19

As for me, I call to God, and the Lord saves me. Evening, morning and noon I cry out in distress, and He hears my voice. He rescues me unharmed from the battle waged against me, even though many oppose me. God, who is enthroned from of old, who does not change—He will hear them and humble them, because they have no fear of God.

Associated Scriptures:

So do not fear, for I am with you; do not be dismayed, for I am your God. I will strengthen you and help you; I will uphold you with My righteous right hand (Isaiah 41:10).

But you remain the same, and Your years will never end (Psalm 102:27).

This is the confidence we have in approaching God: that if we ask anything according to His will, He hears us (1 John 5:14).

I love the Lord, for He heard my voice; He heard my cry for mercy. Because He turned His ear to me, I will call on Him as long as I live (Psalm 116:1-2).

Correlative Quotes:

David does not intend to return evil for evil. His prayer arises from the heart of a pious lover of God, and not from a vengeful despot (*oppressor*).[101] – Kroll

Expressing his confidence in the Lord, David said the Lord saves me. Knowing this, he would continue to call out to Him in his distress, for the Lord, who redeems him in battle, would hear him. God, the sovereign ruler, here's the prayers of His own; He also hears and knows about the violence of the wicked. Having No Fear of God, they are defeated by the lord. Included among those who do not fear God was David's

---

[101] William Michael Kroll, Psalms, Liberty Bble Commentary, The Old-Time Gospel Hour, Lynchburg, Virginia, P. 1049.

companion, who broke his covenant and became deceptively destructive. This *friend's* talk was smooth and soothing but not animosity was in his heart.[102] – Walvoord and Zuck

While it's normal for us to hope for a quick way of escape, and important for us to understand our feelings and circumstances, it's far more important to look up to God and ask for His help. David could no longer lead an army into battle, but he was able to pray that God would defeat the rebel forces, and God answered his prayers. David used Jehovah, the covenant name of God, when he said, "The Lord will save me" (v. 16, NASB). The Jews did have stated hours of prayer (Dan. 6:10; Acts 3:1), but "evening, morning, and at noon" (v. 17) means that David was praying all day long! He no doubt also prayed at night (v. 10). David was certain that the Lord would hear him and rescue him because He was enthroned in heaven and in complete control. David's throne was in danger, but God's throne was secure (9:7–8; 29:10; 74:12).

Author's Notes:

INTRODUCTION: WHEN IT'S THE RIGHT TIME TO PRAY

There is no right time to pray. But there is no wrong time either. 1 Thessalonians 5:17 encourages us to *Pray without ceasing*. We should be thinking about and talking to God continually. However, we should limit the verbal Godly communication to our minds. Otherwise, we will receive some odd looks from those around us.

With all the distractions and interruptions in today's society, it has become more and more challenging to focus on conversation with God or even time to have structured prayer. It therefore behooves us to establish habits of praying. Specific times to pray will help us remember how important it is to talk with God. He wants to hear from us. Our needs are important to Him. The NIV uses the concept of need 77 times. The term needs is used 25 additional times. We are needy people.

The timing of prayer can vary depending on individual preferences and differing daily routines.

---

[102] Walvoord and Zuck, The Bible Knowledge Commentary, O. T., Ibid., P. 835.

MORNING PRAYER:

Many people start their day with prayer, expressing gratitude for a new day and seeking guidance, strength, and protection for the day ahead. Morning prayers can set a positive tone for the day. We should begin our day by talking to God. Proverbs 3:6 states: *In all your ways acknowledge Him, And He shall direct your paths.* There is no wiser guide than God.

MEALTIME PRAYERS:

God enjoys prayers of thanksgiving. Romans 12:12 requires us to *Be joyful in hope, patient in affliction, faithful in prayer.* Saying grace or offering prayers before meals has been historically common in many cultures and religious traditions. It's an opportunity to give thanks for the food and acknowledge the source of nourishment. Since all things belong to God (Deuteronomy 10:14), we should be thankful for His gifts (Matthew 7:11).

PRAYERS BEFORE SLEEP:

Evening or bedtime prayers are a way to reflect on the day, seek forgiveness for any wrongdoings, and entrust the night to God's care. It can also be a time for self-examination and reflection. Nighttime prayers apply to adults as well as to children. Praying with young ones can establish a life-long habit.

Our God is pleased by our prayers: *The sacrifice of the wicked is an abomination to the Lord, but the prayer of the upright is His delight* (Proverbs 15:8).

PRAYERS DURING ORGANIZED GROUP STUDIES OR SUNDAY WORSHIP:

Attending group events to study God's word, church social events, or Sunday church services often includes one or more prayers as part of the worship experience. These services should also include prayers of confession, intercession, and thanksgiving. Using a variety of types of prayer may not meet everyone's needs, but we should practice inclusion. A few of these prayers would include:

The Lord's prayer: Matthew 6:9-13 and the 23rd Psalm.

Number 6:24-26: *The Lord bless you and keep you; the Lord make his face shine on you and be gracious to you; the Lord turn his face toward you and give you peace.*

Psalm 25:4-5: *Make me to know your ways, O Lord; teach us your paths. Lead us in your truth and teach us, for you are the God of our salvation; for you we wait all the day long.*

PRAYERS IN TIMES OF TROUBLE:

Many people turn to prayer in times of crisis, when they face difficulties, or when they need guidance, strength, or comfort. Such prayers are often spontaneous and heartfelt.

Psalm 37:1-4 teaches us to depend completely on God for His protection against affliction: *Fret not yourself because of evildoers; be not envious of wrongdoers! For they will soon fade like the grass and wither like the green herb. Trust in the Lord, and do good; dwell in the land and befriend faithfulness. Delight yourself in the Lord, and he will give you the desires of your heart.*

DAILY DEVOTIONS:

Many Christians incorporate daily devotional times into their schedules,. These special times with God may include reading, meditating on God's Word for understanding or direction, or engaging in prayer. These can happen at any time that is convenient for the individual. Scheduled times help to make prayer habitual and assure we are staying in communication with the Maker.

PRAYERS FOR SPECIAL OCCASIONS:

People often pray on special occasions, such as weddings, funerals, baptisms, and other significant life events. The speaker will tailor the prayer to the occasion's purpose and significance. When praying in public for these formal ceremonies, try to use scripture in the prayer. These events represent one of many reasons why memorizing scripture is vital for all believers. Psalm 119:11 (NKJV) says: *Your word have I hidden in my heart, that I might not sin again You.*

PRAYERS IN TIMES OF GRATITUDE:

For those whom He foreknew, He also predestined to become conformed to the image of His Son, so that He would be the firstborn among many brethren (Romans 8:29).

The most common prayers seem to ask God for some needs, blessings, or the needs of others. We hear a few prayers demonstrating gratitude for our position in Christ and giving thanks to God for our status in Christ Jesus. As God's children by His selection, we should be grateful to God and thank Him regularly for our salvation. It is not something we deserved (Ephesians 2:8-9).

PRAYERS FOR OTHERS:

I urge, then, first of all, that petitions, prayers, intercession and thanksgiving be made for all people— for kings and all those in authority, that we may live peaceful and quiet lives in all godliness and holiness. This is good, and pleases God our Savior, who wants all people to be saved and to come to a knowledge of the truth (1 Timothy 2:1-4).

Therefore, confess your sins to each other and pray for each other so that you may be healed. The prayer of a righteous person is powerful and effective (James 5:16).

Taking time to pray for others, their well-being, and their needs is another crucial aspect of prayer. Take every opportunity to pray for someone in need.

Ultimately, when you should pray depends on your relationship with the Spirit, spiritual practices, and individual circumstances. However, having a prayer plan helps establish a prayer practice. Praying often and consistently must become the disciple's goal. Prayer represents an accessible means of connecting with God, your friends and neighbors, and those who enter your life only momentarily. It will help them to find guidance, comfort, and a sense of purpose in their lives.

THE IMPORTANCE OF TIMING IN PRAYER

They were also to stand every morning to thank and praise the Lord. They were to do the same in the evening (1 Chronicles 23:30)

The timing of prayer is a significant aspect of the practice, and it carries various implications and importance in a person's spiritual life. Here are several reasons why timing in prayer is necessary:

SETTING PRIORITIES:

Allocating specific times for prayer underscores its importance in your life. By dedicating time to prayer, you acknowledge its significance and prioritize your relationship with God above other activities. Often in scripture, God has required specific times and places for praying.

DISCIPLINE AND CONSISTENCY:

Establishing a regular prayer schedule helps build discipline and consistency in your spiritual life and for life in general. Other areas need regularly scheduled events to run smoothly. Just as you set aside time for work, family, and other commitments, dedicating time for prayer fosters a routine of spiritual growth and connection with God.

AVOIDING DISTRACTIONS:

Choosing the right time and the best place for prayer can help minimize distractions. Early morning or late in the evening may be quieter times when you can focus more on your conversation with God without interruptions. Experiencing private prayer time also involves finding a secluded place for prayer to protect from outside disturbances. Oh, and turn off the cell phone for additional inner peace and external quiet.

MENTAL AND EMOTIONAL STATE:

The timing of prayer can coincide with different mental and emotional states. Morning prayers can be a way to start the day with a fresh mind and a clear focus on God. Prayers during a quick lunch might resolve unwanted morning issues or thanksgiving for early-day blessings. Evening prayers can help you reflect on the day and seek God's guidance and peace before bedtime.

ALIGNING WITH SCRIPTURE:

Many biblical figures, including Jesus, had specific times set aside for prayer. Jesus often withdrew to pray early in the morning (Mark 1:35). By following this example, you align your prayer life with the patterns found in Scripture. One of the important theme of Scripture asks us to follow Christ's example (John 14:12).

SPIRITUAL PREPAREDNESS:

Praying at certain times can prepare your heart and mind for specific events or challenges. For instance, praying before a significant meeting or a challenging task can help you seek God's guidance and peace. However, we must have prepared before we pray for success.

COMMUNITY AND CORPORATE PRAYER:

Timing can also be important when participating in corporate or communal prayer. Attending worship services, prayer meetings, or gatherings at specific times allows you to unite with fellow believers when they pray. Habitual prayer prepares us for unexpected opportunities.

RESPONSE TO PROMPTINGS:

Sometimes, we may feel prompted by the Holy Spirit to pray at a particular moment. His promptings to pray when you feel a strong need can be powerful and spiritually enriching. Prayer at meal times, for instance, allows you to express gratitude for the provisions of food and sustenance, recognizing God's role as the provider. We never know when the Spirit will provide an opportunity for us to pray a specific prayer.

Spiritual Application:

The importance of timing in prayer lies in its ability to structure your spiritual life, cultivate consistency, minimize distractions, and align with biblical examples. Always be prepared to pray.

Lessons within the Lesson:

List the thought-provoking verses or statements that spoke to you in this chapter.

Which statement may have the utmost impact on your prayer life?

How will your prayer life change because of this statement?

List the steps you will take to make the changes necessary to strengthen your prayer life.

31: QUESTION 5: WHAT DO WE PRAY FOR?

Luke 11:9-10

Opening Prayer:

Our God and Lord of all Life, I come before You humbly, acknowledging the challenges I sometimes face when I don't know what to pray. There are moments when a heart is overwhelmed with burdens and becomes clouded. My mind sees only confusion, and I grow restless. I am unsure of the words to express my needs. In those times, Lord, I lean on the promise of Your help. The Holy Spirit intercedes for me with groanings too deep for words (Romans 8:26).

I thank You for assurance of Your presence. Even when my prayers are silent, You hear the cries of my heart. Father, I ask for your guidance. Grant Me discernment and clarity when I seek Your will in my prayers. Help me to discern Your will among the noisy life challenges. Teach me to trust in Your sovereignty, knowing You work all things for good for those who love You (Romans 8:28). Thank You for the privilege of coming before Your throne of grace, even in my weakness. In the name of Your Son, Jesus Christ, who taught Me to pray and whose name we bring our petitions, I offer this prayer. Amen.

Today's Bible Verse*: **Luke 11:9-10***

So I say to you: Ask and it will be given to you; seek and you will find; knock and the door will be opened to you. For everyone who asks receives; he who seeks finds; and to him who knocks, the door will be opened.

Associated Scriptures:

> *You are my hiding place; you will protect me from trouble and surround me with songs of deliverance* (Psalm 32:7).

> *But I pray to you, O Lord, in the time of your favor; in your great love, O God, answer me with your sure salvation. Rescue me from the mire, do not let me sink; deliver me from those who hate me, from the deep waters. Do not let the floodwaters engulf me or the depths swallow me up or the pit close its mouth over me. Answer me, O Lord, out of the goodness of your love; in your great mercy turn to me* (Psalm 69:13-16).

> *But you, dear friends, build yourselves up in your most holy faith and pray in the Holy Spirit. 21 Keep yourselves in God's love as you wait for the mercy of our Lord Jesus Christ to bring you to eternal life* (Jude 20-21).

Correlative Quotes:

The first mark of a follower of Christ is that he believes his Lord. We do not follow the Lord at all if we raise any questions upon points whereupon He speaks positively. Though a doctrine should be surrounded with ten thousand difficulties, the *ipse dixit* (He said it Himself) of the Lord Jesus sweeps them all away, as far as true Christians are concerned. Our Master's declaration is all the argument we want, "I say unto you," is our logic. Reason! We see you at your best in Jesus, for He is made of God unto us wisdom. He cannot err. He cannot lie, and if He says, "I say unto you," there is an end of all debate.[103] – Spurgeon

This does not absolve us from intensity in prayer. After all, we can guarantee the reality and sincerity of our desire only by the passion with which we pray. But it does mean this, that we are not wringing gifts from an unwilling God, but going to one who knows our needs better than we know them ourselves and

---

[103] Charles Spurgeon, Prayer Certified Of Success, Message # 1091, P. 2.

whose heart towards us is the heart of generous love.[104] – Barclay

Jesus applies the story by stressing three words in regard to prayer - "Ask... Seek... Knock." It is for our own soul's good that we become earnest in our supplications, pouring out our hearts in unremitting intercession, literally storming the gate of the storehouse of blessing until the answer comes. God will never deny the prayer of faith. "Ask," "Seek," "Knock," are degrees of importunity. As we continue to besiege the throne of grace we shall be moved to heart-searching and to self-judgment, that thus we may pray according to the will of God.[105] – Ironside

Author's Notes:

INTRODUCTION

Luke 11:9-10 contains a powerful teaching from Jesus regarding prayer. In this passage, Jesus shares several aspects showing wisdom on how His disciples and believers should approach God in prayer. These verses are part of a larger discourse (Luke 11:1-13) where Jesus instructs His followers on the principles impacting effective, fervent prayer. This section of Scripture also includes Luke's version of the Lord's prayer (compare with Matthew 6:9-13). Jesus also discusses the persistence of asking God (Luke 11:5-8) and the goodness of God in response to our prayers (Luke 11:11-13).

CONTEXT OF CHRIST'S WORDS

In the context of Luke 11, Jesus is responding to His disciples' request to teach them how to pray. He follows these verses with the Lord's Prayer (Luke 11:2-4), providing a practical model for prayer. The teaching on asking, seeking, and knocking serves as a foundation for understanding the principles of effective prayer.

The Lord's teaching on prayer arises from a broader observation of this text. His followers desire to learn how to pray. However, they also want

---

[104] William Barclay, We Have Seen the Lord, Westminster John Knox Press, Louisville Kentucky, Used by permission, Fair Use Authorization, Section 107, of the Copyright Law, P. 21.

[105] H. A. Ironside, Luke, Loizeaux Brothers, New York, Used by permission, Fair Use Authorization, Section 107, of the Copyright Law, P. 243.

to know what to ask for. Following the Lord's Prayer, Jesus further expounds on the subject of prayer, which includes the verses in question, Luke 11:9-10. Their desire to learn how to pray kindles the remarks of the Messiah. His answer is all-inclusive. We may ask for anything in His name.

CHRIST'S TEACHING ON PRAYER

Christ's words contain a concise yet profound lesson on prayer. In these verses, Jesus uses imperatives *ask, seek, and knock* emphasizing the active and persistent nature of prayer. He assures His disciples that those who engage in earnest, persevering prayer will receive, find, and have doors opened to them. God answers the prayers of those who live in love and obedience to Him (James 5:16).

CHRIST'S UNIVERSAL APPLICABILITY

The Savior's teaching in this section of Luke is not limited to His immediate disciples. As in most cases in scripture, they apply universally to all believers. The phrase, For everyone who asks receives, in verse 10 underscores the inclusive nature of His remarks. These words highlight His willingness to respond to prayer. They affect everyone who approaches Him in faith (Matthew 21:22), obedience (John 15:7), and according to His will (1 Thessalonians 5:15-18).

CHRIST'S WORDS AND THEIR THEOLOGICAL SIGNIFICANCE:

These verses in Luke 11:11-13 emphasize the importance of persistence and faith in prayer. They affirm the idea that God desires His children to actively engage in seeking His will and provision through prayer. For example, what father would give you a snake when you ask for a fish? This seemly ridiculous question makes the point clear: God will give believers what they need even if it is not exactly what they ask for.

From a theological perspective, these verses underscore the importance of active engagement in prayer *ask, seek,* and *knock* are necessary ingredients to answered prayers. While they do not guarantee God will grant every request requested, they convey one amazing truth: He listens to and responds to the heartfelt prayers of His children according to His wisdom and purposes. The apostle John states in 1 John 5:14-15: This is the confidence we have in approaching God: that if we ask anything according to his will, he hears us. And if we know that he hears us — whatever we ask — we know that we have what we asked of him.

168

CHRIST'S PROGRESSION

The three imperatives represent a progression. Asking is the initial step. Naturally, we must ask if we are to receive anything. Even children learn to ask early in life. Seeking involves a more intense effort. The man seeking food knew his neighbor had three loaves of bread. Therefore, he sought help where it was available. Knocking requires persistence and determination.

In the example Jesus gives us in Luke 11:5-8, the man's doggedness brings home the bread. If the man had not endured, he and his friends would have gone to bed hungry. This progression highlights the importance of persistence in prayer.

CHRIST'S ASSURANCE

Jesus assures those who ask, seek, and knock. They will receive, find, and have the door open to them. This assurance underscores God's willingness to respond to the earnest prayers of His children. Trust also comes into play in this narrative. We must believe, however, that those who seek answers to prayer must trust God to provide for their needs.

UNIVERSAL APPLICATION THROUGH CHRIST:

His use of the word *everyone* in verse 10 emphasizes how God's teaching on prayer applies to all believers. It implies His willingness to answer prayer is not limited to a select few but extends to all who approach Him in faith. All believers, therefore, have access to His promises through the Spirit.

Ephesians 2:18 teaches: *For through him we both have access to the Father by one Spirit.*

IN SUMMARY

While in prayer, believers can bring a wide range of requests and concerns to God. The Bible guides what we can pray for.

WORSHIP AND THANKSGIVING:

Start by praising and thanking God for who He is and the blessings you have received. Express gratitude for His love, mercy, and provision.

CONFESSION AND FORGIVENESS:

Confess your sins and shortcomings, seeking God's forgiveness and cleansing through the atonement of Jesus Christ. Acknowledge your need for His grace and mercy.

GUIDANCE AND WISDOM:

Seek God's guidance in decision-making, asking for His wisdom and discernment. Pray for clarity and understanding in life's challenges and choices.

STRENGTH AND PERSEVERANCE:

Pray for strength to endure trials, difficulties, and temptations. Ask for the perseverance to remain faithful in the face of adversity.

HEALING AND RESTORATION:

Pray for physical, emotional, and spiritual healing for yourself and others who are sick or suffering. Trust in God's power to bring restoration and wholeness.

PROTECTION AND SAFETY:

Pray for God's protection over yourself, your loved ones, and others in dangerous or challenging situations. Seek His divine intervention in times of crisis.

INTERCESSION FOR OTHERS:

Lift up the needs and concerns of others in your prayers. Intercede on behalf of friends, family, the community, and the world. Pray for their well-being, salvation, and specific needs.

SALVATION AND OUTREACH:

Pray for the salvation of those who do not know Jesus Christ as their Savior. Ask God to open doors for evangelism and mission work to spread the Gospel.

UNITY AND PEACE:

Pray for unity and reconciliation in relationships, families, churches, and communities. Seek God's peace in conflict or division.

FRUITFULNESS AND SPIRITUAL GROWTH:

Pray for spiritual growth, maturity, and bearing fruit in your own life and the lives of others. Ask God to help you grow in faith, love, and holiness.

CONTENTMENT AND PROVISION:

Pray for contentment with what you have and trust in God's provision for your needs. Seek His guidance in managing resources wisely.

PRAISE FOR GOD'S PROMISES:

Thank God for His promises in Scripture and claim them in your prayers. Trust in His faithfulness to fulfill His Word.

SURRENDER AND YIELDING:

Surrender your will to God's will. Ask Him to shape your desires and align them with His purposes.

COMMUNITY AND FELLOWSHIP:

Pray for the strength and unity of your Christian community, including your church. Seek opportunities for mutual encouragement and growth.

Spiritual Application:

CHRIST'S PRACTICAL APPLICATION:

The practical application of Luke 11:9-10 encourages believers to approach prayer with confidence and persistence. It reminds us to actively seek God's will, provision, and guidance through ongoing and heartfelt communication with Him.

Luke 11:9-10 serves as a pivotal moment in Jesus' teaching on prayer, offering guidance and assurance to His disciples and all who seek to deepen their relationship with God through prayer. These verses invite us to approach God with faith, persistence, and expectancy in our prayers, knowing that He hears and responds to the cries of His children.

OUR FLEXIBILITY AND SPONTANEITY:

Having set prayer times is crucial, it is also vital to remain flexible and open to spontaneous prayer throughout the day. Since prayer is talking to God, it should be natural for us to speak to Him at any time, in any situation. Moments of gratitude, intercession, or praise can arise unexpectedly, and you should feel free to respond in prayer as the Spirit leads. Spontaneous prayer may be the most powerful weapon in God's prayer arsenal. Like any emergency responder, we must prepare to pray when God or humanity calls.

Remember that prayer is a conversation with God, and you can bring any concerns or desires of your heart to Him. Be open to the leading of the Holy Spirit and the prompting of God's Word as you pray. Additionally, while it's appropriate to pray for specific needs, maintain an attitude of submission to God's sovereign will, trusting that He knows what is best for you and others.

Finally, as a result of the teaching regarding prayer in Luke 11:9-10, believers should continually express thanksgiving in their communication with God. It highlights the assurance that God responds to the earnest prayers of His children and emphasizes the universal applicability of this teaching to all believers. We can't praise and thank our Lord enough for His response to our continuing needs. Psalms 40:17 (NKJV) says: *But I am poor and needy, yet the Lord thinks upon me. We are a needy people. God is a gracious giver.*

Lessons within the Lesson:

List the thought-provoking verses or statements that spoke to you in this chapter.

Which statement may have the utmost impact on your prayer life?

How will your prayer life change because of this statement?

List the steps you will take to make the changes necessary to strengthen your prayer life.

Made in the USA
Las Vegas, NV
14 September 2023

77510782R00095